Keith Hill is a New Zealand writer whose work explores the intersection of mysticism, history, science, religion and psychology. His books include *The God Revolution*, *Striving To Be Human*, and *Practical Spirituality*, each of which won the Ashton Wylie Award, New Zealand's premiere prize for spiritual writing. Since 2008 he has been working with fellow channeller Peter Calvert to present new metaphysical and psychospiritual perspectives relevant to twenty-first century spiritual seekers.

BOOKS BY KEITH HILL

NON-FICTION

The New Mysticism

The God Revolution

Striving To Be Human

CHANNELLED BOOKS

What is Really Going On?

Where Do I Go When I Meditate?

Experimental Spirituality

Practical Spirituality

Psychological Spirituality

CLASSICS OF WORLD MYSTICISM

The Bhagavad Gita: A New Poetic Version

Interpretations of Desire:
Mystical Love Poems by Ibn 'Arabi

I Cannot Live Without You:
Selected Poetry of Mirabai and Kabir

Psalms of Exile and Return:
A Journey of Spiritual Integration and Healing

FICTION

The Ecstasy of Cabeza de Vaca

Puck of the Starways

Blue Kisses

CHANNELLED WITH PETER CALVERT

The Matapaua Conversations

The Kosmic Web

How Did I End Up Here?

Your life plan, purpose and digging
into the subtleties of your existence

Keith Hill

First published by Attar Books 2018
Copyright © Keith Hill 2018
The moral rights of the author have been asserted.

Paperback ISBN 978-0-9951059-6-6
Ebook ISBN 978-0-9951059-7-3

Cover designed by Abigail Kerr

Attar Books
www.attarbooks.com   www.experimentalspirituality.net

Contents

Jumping into the deep end

HOW DID WE END UP where we are, living the life we lead, being with the people most important to us? How did we come to have the advantages and problems we have and not others? Why do we have this career, that partner, those possibilities, and not another career, partner or set of possibilities? These questions are among life's great imponderables. Three answers are most commonly offered.

The first is that God is whistling the tune we're dancing to. God created the world, then us, and plonked us into the middle of it. So whatever happens, God is responsible. Naturally, this explanation gets complicated when you add in choice, doing good and avoiding sin, and dealing with the consequences of what we do. Nonetheless, in this view ultimately it's all God's doing.

The second answer is we're here because of chance. Our parents got together due to some random sequence of events, and another random interaction of DNA in their genes created the person we are. Then, once we were born, a bunch of other factors influenced who we became, including key childhood experiences, social programming, and the cultural norms that dominated where we were raised. But that's all chance too, because who knows how anything will turn out? Bottom line: we're an accidentally created being living in a random world.

The third answer is that whatever happens is meant to be. This is for those who suspect more is going on than the pure chance view suggests, but they don't want to get caught up in the religious stuff.

This view accepts there could be some kind of organisation going on behind the scenes, but we can't see what it is. What will be, will be. So we should just accept our lot and get on with it.

What these three responses share is that they don't attempt to grapple with the deeper causes of what is going on in our lives. They don't delve into why we are who we are, why we have these particular opportunities and problems, why that person entered our life at a key moment, or why our life isn't working out how we want, no matter what we try. Not only don't these responses take us into the depths of our life, they accept that we *can't know* what's happening in the depths, so really there's no point trying to find out.

I find this highly unsatisfactory. What if there *is* more to us being here? What if we *can* identify the influences that shape the path our life takes? And what if we *are* engaged in the selection of those influences? That's what this book explores.

As with the first two books in this series, this is a channelled text. From friends I gathered a range of questions around the theme of why our life is the way it is, then put them to the non-embodied guides I have been in communication with since 2011. Because the guides incarnated innumerable times themselves, they know from the inside what being human is all about. Drawing on their own experiences, and their subsequent post-incarnational observations, they focus on what is most relevant to our unravelling the mystery of who we are, where we are, and why we're doing what we are.

Where the answers end up is often unexpected. The responses offer practical psychological advice, guidance on how to use self-enquiry to dig into our deep nature, and information on how our life plan ties it all together. There's also mind-expanding metaphysical material that reframes big life questions. In places, it's a wild ride. Buckle up. I hope it takes you someplace you find both stimulating and useful.

—Keith Hill, Auckland, June 2018

Question 1

Why am I here?

My question is basic. You keep saying we're here to experience and learn, and it's a process that helps us grow spiritually. I can appreciate that as a general statement. But I want to get more specific. What is my purpose in this life? What should I be doing? How can I discover why I'm here?

THE GUIDES RESPOND:

Once again we welcome everyone to these discussions of spiritual matters. Before answering the question, we wish to comment on the process by which this series of books is being produced.

We acknowledge our scribe, who is diligently dedicating time and energy to our communications. These books would not exist in their present form without his close attention. We also acknowledge those who provide questions. Without their input significant information would not be included. While we have begun each of the books in this series with a plan, intending to share specific ideas and perspectives, the material is far from locked down. Some questions have taken the conversations—because at heart that is what these books are—into territory that to us is unintended, even surprising. The result is that we are very satisfied with the level of information we have shared.

Naturally, there is much else we intend to say should this series continue. The sharing involves a to and fro process. As a result, these books are not pre-constructed packages of information that we regurgitate, as occurs in university lecture halls. Instead, they involve what our scribe calls an organic process. It is a responsive process. We respond to questions, and questioners in turn respond to our answers with further questions. So as we begin this new book, while we have in mind certain information we wish to pass on, exactly how that information will be expressed, which related ideas will be explored, and even where we will collectively end up, remains open. Thus we acknowledge that whatever comes to be included is the result of a three-way communication process, between those who ask questions, us, and our scribe.

This is also how an individual life goes. When you are born no one knows where precisely your life will lead. There is a plan, but no one either on Earth or in the spiritual realm knows how much of the plan will be realised in a particular life. That is the reason each life keeps everyone involved on their toes. You only find out what will happen during the course of your life by living your life. That is the wonder of incarnation. That is its mystery.

It is because people are aware a mystery beats at the heart of their life that they question their existence. We say this because, like you, we have lived many lives and so are speaking from experience when we say it is common for people to feel that a veil hides the deepest aspects of their life. Often this feeling includes the intuition that some kind of plan is in place.

Another way of saying this is that people intuit that their life has a greater purpose. However vaguely they feel it, and however their feeling is expressed, people want to know living isn't a matter of carrying on just because they are here. People want to be assured that their life has a deeper purpose. They want to know there's a reason they've been born at this time, in this body and this family, into this culture, and into the particular circumstances that govern their life. The reason people ask deep questions is to get to the bottom of it all, to lift the veil and penetrate the mystery hidden at the centre of their life.

The world's religions have addressed these questions, offering their own answers. Broadly speaking, those answers are not fine-grained. That is, they don't address the specifics of an individual's life. They are much more general responses, using words such as salvation, freedom, transcendence, and heaven and hell. For many this general level of response is sufficient and they stop asking further. In contrast, the question asked here seeks to move beyond the general to the personal: What is *my* purpose? What should *I* be doing? Happily, this is the level we also wish to address.

Our perspective is that before you were born you put a plan in place. The standard religious perspective is that God has drawn up your life plan. That doesn't agree with our perceptions. Our view is that *you* have formulated your life plan. *You* have chosen your life's purpose. What *you* decide creates your life's meaning.

The complication is that lives often don't pan out as planned. There are many mitigating factors that alter the course of a life. You may not do everything you planned to. A task may take much longer than anticipated. You might even choose to go off plan. Others who agreed—before you both were born—to meet up with you and carry out a joint task may be detained, diverted or change their mind. In addition, accidents happen. Unforeseen events may result in people turning up before or after the agreed time. Just as this happens during the course of your day, so it happens during the course of your life. We add that devils and their cohort are not responsible for any of this. There are no evil players subverting your plans. There are just people doing what people do, intending something and doing it well, doing it poorly, or not doing it all. Life is that simple. And that complicated.

Of course, the question is asked because you are very aware that whatever the plan is, you're not in on it. You can't see what's behind the veil. You don't know why you and those you care for decide to do this rather than that. It is this lack of knowledge, this mystery, that has given rise to the question in the first place: why am I here?

In this context, in a book for general reading, it is not possible for us to tell individuals exactly what is going on in their life, nor identify what their life plan involves. And even if it was possible, we wouldn't say. Just as you find out what the future holds by living long enough for the future to arrive, so the only way to understand what is happening at the heart of your life is to lift the veil yourself. If you really want to understand what your life plan involves, *you* have to look behind the flow of events that make up your life's day by day experience.

Accordingly, we suggest that the way to answer the question of why you are here is via a process of self-enquiry. Before you were born you generated a life plan. Over the years since you were born various constricting circumstances and unforeseen events have altered how your life plan has played out, impacting on it to a lesser or a greater extent. Together, your plan, life situations and your choices have shaped the particular circumstances of your life. By closely examining your life, by looking behind the daily flow of what is happening, it is possible to identify the key factors that shape your psychological makeup, your decision-making processes, and why you do what you do.

It is by adopting a process of self-enquiry, and seriously following it through, that it becomes quite possible for you to lift the veil, shine a light into the mysterious heart of your existence, and identify the contours of your life as you intended it to be.

Question 2

I have a life plan?
That's no comfort at all!

You said I have a life plan. And that I prepared it before I was born. So before I was born I chose what I would do with my life, who I will or won't marry, how many kids I'll have, even where I'm living right now? Is my life nailed down that much? I'm confused because it suggests that everything important in my life is pre-destined, so I have no choice. Even more confusing, you say I have organised my own life, yet I have no idea where my life is headed, and there are so many things happening around me that I have no control over. So what you're saying is mystifying, not comforting!

THE GUIDES RESPOND:

We begin answering this question by offering a general observation. Human beings have a natural tendency to exaggerate. Whether their life goes well or badly, it is natural to go to extremes and become very happy or very upset. In reality things are hardly ever that bad. Or good. Life just plays out as it will, and whatever happens, however things turn out, soon enough you are looking at them in the rearview mirror. That's just the way human existence is.

Of course, we know that is not how it seems when you are living through pleasurable or tough times. That is why we said human beings have a natural tendency to exaggerate. The tendency is natural because a core requirement of embodiment is that the experience of being human be real. Accordingly, incarnation involves identification and attachment. People identify with the state of having a body and all that involves, and get attached to people, situations, objects, and everything else that goes with living a human existence. Identification and attachment ensure that experiences count, that they make a powerful impression on you. These impressions then provide what you need to extract life lessons, which in turn enable you to grow. So while exaggeration is a natural outcome of this learning process, nonetheless it occurs because you are deeply embedded in the particulars of your life.

How is this relevant to answering the question? It is relevant because if you are always caught up in the process of living, if you continue to react to what is on your plate day by day, you won't be able to see what has occurred behind the scenes to get you into the situations that now dominate your life. To answer your question for yourself, which is our recommendation, you have to learn to disentangle yourself from the immediate moment, step back, and take a wider view of what is going on around you, to you, and within you.

We put this question into that basket. By which we mean, saying you have no choice, that you lack control of your life, that everything is pre-destined—excuse our language here, but that is all poppycock. You know perfectly well that your life is as you chose it. To say otherwise, that you are helpless, that you know nothing, is an exaggeration. The real reason you don't understand your own life plan is because you have not enquired sufficiently into the circumstances of your own life. You haven't enquired into your own psychological make-up. And you especially haven't sufficiently tried to grapple with the deep aspects of your own identity.

So we suggest that in order to find your own answer to what is going on in your life, set aside your feelings of being confused, or that you're being left out, or whatever other emotion that dominates your feelings about yourself, and instead get serious about your own deep nature. Do that and much that is confusing will become clear. Not everything will become clear immediately, we admit that, because human identity is a complex, multilayered construct, but certainly enough will become clear to allow you to see that, yes, you do have significant control, and no, you are not helpless in the face of powerful people and situations, even though, when you are encountering them, they seem to be overwhelming. Nothing is insurmountable. Everything about your human existence will eventually be clarified. The key is to keep accumulating insights into the specifics of your existence.

Our view of human spirituality is multi-faceted. You are a spiritual identity occupying a human body. It takes many lives to come to terms with this situation. Then more lives to find the spiritual core within you. Then yet more lives to learn to express your spiritual core in the circumstances of daily life. Too many things to list here have to be learned during the course of becoming spiritual. Being religious, being an atheist, being a mystic, a martyr, a sceptic—you will adopt all these roles and many more as you work through how best to express yourself in a human world that veers between being harsh, beautiful, difficult, astonishing, loving, traumatising, mysterious, and surprising. And it *is* surprising, despite you having organised the major events you will experience during the course of your current life.

We have discussed at length elsewhere what is involved in a life plan, particularly in the *Channelled Spirituality Series* of books, so we won't go over that ground again here. However, we will reiterate that the whole point of having a life plan is not to lead people to feel coerced or that they have to follow a pre-laid path from which they cannot deviate. As we have stated frequently, and undoubtedly will repeat, you have choice. If you really wanted you could ditch your job, leave your relationships, and dismantle all you have organised for your life. This is a choice you could make if you really want to. So any complaints that you are hemmed in and helpless are wide of the mark. The fact is, few people have the courage to ditch everything and totally re-organise their life. We do not say this disparagingly, because for most people there is no need to do so. Living through the current circumstances of your life, working through the liabilities and responsibilities that are entwined into your life, is what you have signed up to do.

As far as being confused is concerned, that is another inevitable consequence of embodiment. Human perception is narrow, whereas you need a wide view to perceive all the complexities of interlinked factors that contribute to you being where you currently are. The psychological processes of identification and attachment focus your attention on your day-to-day experience of being human, resulting in you not being able to stand back and take that recommended wide view. Between lives you do have the opportunity to adopt a wider view. And as you evolve, life by life, your view becomes incrementally wider and deeper. This means that your spiritual self sees more than you do at your current human level. It also means you can draw on what your spiritual self knows in order to understand what is happening to you in this life and how you ended up where you are.

This is what the process of becoming spiritual is all about: drawing on what your spiritual self knows and using it to infuse how you are living your life. In saying this we are addressing those who have reached the point where they seriously wish to perceive what lies behind the veil that hangs across their awareness and prevents them from understanding the who, where, what and why of their existence.

In that sense, our advice here is directed towards those whose view of themselves is maturing, for those for whom living life up close and personal, as we have described it elsewhere, is no longer enough. For whatever reason, and there are many, you now wish to adopt a wider view, a deeper view, and see what is really happening in the particulars of your life. We reiterate, that is who we are specifically addressing here. And it is to these people that we recommend a process of self-enquiry.

Question 3

Isn't God, not me, the mystery behind everything?

You talked about there being a mystery at the heart of our life and that we can lift the veil and shine a light into it. Surely, the mystery at the centre of our life is God? Even if God isn't ultimately controlling what happens in my life—and I don't understand why He wouldn't be, because God is the source of everything—surely God is the mystery we are ultimately seeking, and not our own self? Isn't what you're recommending a narcissistic approach to spirituality?

THE GUIDES RESPOND:

Before we can talk about God we need to agree on what concept of God we are addressing. Throughout history human beings have worshipped thousands of gods, all with different names, attributes, and relationships to human beings. To adopt our scribe's language, there are monotheistic concepts of a single God, the polytheistic concept of many gods, the idea that gods embody natural forces, and the notions of city and household gods who protect a single place or family. Many people have a narrow attitude towards God, proclaiming their God all-powerful and above all other gods. Others have a pluralist attitude, accepting all gods as valid for those who believe in them. For our response here, we will focus on just two notions of God: God as creator and the psychological God.

That God is the creator of the world is a belief promoted by all the world's religions. It is a belief with which we concur. However, it comes with a major sticking point. When people first postulated God as creator of the world, they conceived of the world in local terms, as the immediate environment in which they lived, that being jungle, mountains, coast, plains, and so on. When travellers discovered new places their appreciation of what constituted the world expanded and their notion of God as creator of the world expanded correspondingly. Nonetheless, until recent centuries the world remained physically contained and God was thought of as either a super-person who created the world or, in later eras, as an abstract entity or principle who created the world. For millennia that remained the dominate notion: that the world was this planetary environment, and that God, however conceived, created it.

This has become a sticking point today because humanity knows that the world consists not just of this planet, nor this solar system, nor even this galaxy. The concept of world, in its fullest sense, now encompasses billions of galaxies existing within a universe that is little mapped and whose extremities remain unknown. Furthermore, the universe is dominated by dark matter and dark energy, which are called dark because scientists have no idea what they are.

The fact that the notion of a localised world has been exploded, replaced by the notion of an expansive reality which is mostly unknown, means that the notion of God as localised creator has also been exploded. Given the vastness of reality, if God is considered to be the creator of reality, then God is too vast to be conceived. This means that God as creator is not just unknown, it is unknowable. Why unknowable? Because whatever created the vastness of all that is exists at a level that is far beyond what scientists can measure or that the human mind and heart will ever be capable of comprehending.

Is such an unknowable, incomprehensible God the mystery that pulses at the depths of your existence? Certainly, because it pulses in the depths of everything that exists. Is directing your attention towards this mystery going to enhance your understanding of your own spiritual nature? No, it will not. Why not? Because the creator God is too far beyond your powers of perception, and so is too hidden to be comprehended by you.

We don't mean by this that you should ignore God the creator completely. Meditating on the mystery that is the creator God is a worthwhile exercise, as it will give you a sense of how small you are, that you are a miniscule thread in the fabric of all that is. Nonetheless, there is no way to directly interface with the vast, unknowable creator God. And what is unknowable cannot illuminate what is happening to you as you live your life.

Neither is it useful, we add, to pray to the creator God to help you through your difficulties. It exists on a transcendent level of being such that there cannot be any direct interaction between you and God. Of course, this doesn't mean your prayers go unheard. Your prayers are certainly heard by your own spiritual self, and by those in spirit, including soul friends, who care for you.

Whether or not any answer comes when you call out depends on what is happening to you, particularly on whether you really do need help there and then, or whether you are caught up in the moment and so exaggerating how much trouble you are in. As events play out, and as you adjust to circumstances, help will be offered according to what is possible and what you need.

To return to our answer, if the creator God is too far away to hear you, what then? The fact is that throughout history many people have felt that their God was too distant and not answering their calls, so they adjusted their notion of God to a being possessing more human dimensions. Thus you have the notion of God as embodied in Jesus Christ, Krishna, Athena, Isis, Thor, Zeus, and any of the thousands of gods human hearts and minds have invented. We deliberately use the words *human hearts and minds have invented* because the human spirit knows better. Your spiritual self knows that God cannot be squeezed into a human frame. It is your human self that invents human-sized gods with whom to commune. This leads to the notion of the psychological God.

People often feel hurt and lost and that they need help, so they call out to their God. They call out because deep inside they know there is more to their existence than just flesh and blood, that they are more than just a body. The identity who is nearest to them, and who therefore first hears their cry, is their own spiritual self. But few people are brought up to understand this. What they are brought up with instead is a belief in God as the immediate receiver of their prayers and cries for help. Or, to be fair, as the recipient also of their deepest expressions of gratitude. The problem is that it is their spiritual self, not their God, who actually hears their cries and thanks. Nonetheless, they continue to believe in their God over and above their own spiritual self.

What is happening in such a case is that they are projecting a notion of God onto their own spiritual self. That is, they innately sense that something more is present in their lives, and they desire that something more to help them, whether by guiding them, comforting them, reassuring them, or nurturing them. Their spiritual self is certainly able to do these things. But instead of appreciating the reality of their spiritual situation, and so seeking to make contact with their own spiritual self, they call out to the God which they, in most cases, have been brought up to believe in. Accordingly, they project their learned notion of God onto the something more that they sense is in them and around them. So their cry is directed towards an abstract, amorphous, projected notion of God.

This is the psychological God who possesses the characteristics you wish your God to have, combined with what others have taught you God possesses. In this sense, anyone's psychological God is at its heart a projection of their own hopes, fears, imagination, justifications, despair, and whatever else occupies them at a deep psychological level. These qualities are then filtered through learned notions of what God is or is not and can or cannot do.

At this point an aside needs to be made regarding those who do not believe that human beings possess any something more at all. Such people usually not only do not believe in the existence of God, they also reject the notion that they have a spiritual self that existed before their birth and that will continue to exist after their body dies. Like everyone, such people are working through what they believe life by life. Often individuals have to reject all religious beliefs in order to clear their palate, so to speak, before they can taste deeper aspects of reality without their hearts and minds being overwhelmed by other people's projections regarding God. Many people go through such a clearing process during the course of their life, as they come to appreciate the extent to which the beliefs they were taught during childhood are inventions, often fantastical in construct, that are inhibiting their efforts to make the most of their life.

Of course, completely rejecting the "something more" that is their spiritual self, that they have a blank at their core, is as much an act of projection as superimposing God over it. So rejecting the "something more" doesn't signal the end of juggling beliefs for that person. Rather, it is just part of the learning process. It's what people work their way through over the course of many lives. There is nothing wrong with any stance a person takes, whether rational acceptance or rational rejection of God, irrational acceptance or irrational rejection, and the many shades between. It is, as is said, all grist to the mill. Nonetheless, there are a number of points to be made regarding people's projection of a psychological God.

The first is that, as we said earlier, when you call out to your God, who is in fact no more than a projection of your own hopes, fears, desires, etc, this doesn't mean that no one is home to receive your message. You at the level of your spiritual self hear, and you are there to help. So are your close soul friends. So are others, including tutors and teachers, who have taken on the task of caring for you. So you are neither ignored nor abandoned. Be assured of this.

Second, when people cry out to God for help, they are seeking comfort. This is because when people cry out they are in an upset emotional state, so are seeking emotional support. They want to know they are cared for and loved, that someone is looking after them. They especially want to know that in the end everything will be all right.

Incidentally, this is why people use the terms father and mother in relation to God. They want God to provide a parents' love and care. In this situation, people have a psychological God who exists as their projection of the human child-parent relationship onto the something more that they sense is in them and around them. Certainly, it is valid to call out to others when you feel hurt or lost. Yet the limitation in doing so is that children are dependent on others for help, whereas adults take responsibility for themselves. And the spiritual task you are engaged in involves growing spiritually from child to adult. Seeing through and shrugging off the psychological God is a necessary task for everyone as they strive to develop spiritually.

This brings us to the third point. We observed that when people call out to God they usually do so emotionally. They rarely do so intellectually. Yet knowledge of who you are and of how your life came to be as it is is itself a great comfort in times of unease. For that reason we recommend you deconstruct whatever notion you have of God.

The question states that God is at the centre of each person's life, therefore the mystery to be unravelled is God. This is a valid view. However, as we pointed out, God as the creator is beyond human understanding, so must remain a mystery. The God that *is* accessible is your psychological God. In fact, it is not only accessible, it constantly colours your view of the world. And we note that not believing in God is also a form of projection, it is just a negative projection, what could be called a black hole, which equally colours your view of the world and your life in it.

So we agree, yes, by all means seek to unravel the mystery of your psychological God. Analyse how you came to believe what you believe, why this God is constructed as it is in your heart and mind, what your emotional relationship is to this God, and to what degree you project it onto the circumstances of your life. Does its presence make you feel guilty, inadequate, sinful, privileged, blessed or saved? All these are psychological traits you project onto God, onto the world, and onto yourself. Unravelling this mystery is certainly an extremely useful task. In this sense we are recommending that rather than *calling out to* your God, you instead *call out* your God. Deconstruct your psychological God and untangle the mystery that so powerfully impacts on your life.

To address the last part of the question, is doing so narcissistic? Is focussing on your small own self, rather than on the vast isness of God, a narrow, self-absorbed way of conducting yourself through a life on this planet? We will answer this in developmental terms. When you were an infant you understood little to nothing of the adult world. Instead, other things occupied you and took up your attention, like learning how to speak and walk. Similarly, there is a time when you have to focus on the construction of your own self, of your own reality, and of the notions others have taught you. You need to do this in order to deconstruct them, so you may learn about the multi-layered nature of your identity. Only when you understand this will you be able to fully utilise all that you have and are.

You are the greatest mystery in your own life. The depth of who and what you are is hidden from you. Spending time, a lot of time, life times in fact, to unravel this mystery will not just prove gratifying to you, it is an essential part of the task of developing into a responsible adult who has sufficient wisdom to be able to help those others who are still learning to shrug off their own misconceptions and to appreciate the mystery that, deep down, they are.

Question 4

Is there other life in the universe?

I have a tragi-comic perspective that there is much to be gained by accepting, in fact embracing, the great ironies present in life and living. As a result I don't question life very much. But knowing if the universe is completely empty other than us, or if it is teeming with other life, in whatever form, would deeply affect me, and very probably influence my approach to life and my view of it. So is there, or isn't there, other life in this universe?

THE GUIDES RESPOND:

This is a very useful question, as it introduces a number of issues pertinent to what we intend to discuss in this book. First a little background is required. Technological developments are enabling astrophysicists and their ilk to peer ever deeper into space and learn how stars and galaxies form and to gain insights into how the universe is evolving. This exploration is driven by people's curiosity. Curiosity has clearly been to humanity's benefit. It has led to conceptual breakthroughs that have transformed how human beings view the world and technological breakthroughs that have radically altered how human beings live on this planet. However, a number of restrictions exist that must be acknowledged in relation to the advancement of human knowledge of the universe.

The first is that when human scientists peer out into intergalactic space, they do so from the viewpoint of this planet. This is a major limitation. Certainly, satellite probes have been sent out to observe the solar system's outer planets and collect data about them. These have enabled scientists to get much closer to Saturn and Jupiter and their moons than they could achieve by observing them from the Earth. However, what they are doing is the equivalent of sending a drone carrying a camera up the street to look into the backyard of the corner store. All that exists across this planet beyond the corner store remains unobserved. Similarly for human scientists, their satellite probes are unable to gather information from the edges of the solar system, let alone observe what is occurring beyond the solar system, in the vastness of intergalactic space. So these probes don't alter the situation that limits human observational capabilities: the fact that scientists peer into the universe from this planet, and that single viewpoint is intrinsically restricted.

To put this situation into perspective, it is like trying to learn all about the Himalayas while observing from just one spot. Much can be learned from this one spot, of course. But much more will not be. For example, it could be that a major arterial highway exists in a valley on the other side of a ridge. The ridge can be seen by a powerful telescope, but because the highway is out of direct line of sight its existence will always remain unknown. Let's say the observers sometimes hear a faint buzzing, about which they theorise. But lacking observational data, their theories are necessarily guesswork. If those studying the Himalyas have never seen a motor vehicle, and so lack the concept of a highway, none would have the slightest idea of what is really causing the occasional buzzing they hear.

This situation could be further likened to there being an intergalactic throughway on the far side of Alpha Centauri. However, the vehicles are too small and moving too fast to register on the comparatively crude measuring devices operated by Earth-bound scientists observing from over four million light years away. We are not saying this is actually the case, or that there is such an intergalactic highway. What we are offering is a metaphor to illustrate our point. Having a perspective limited to the surface of this planet, and using measuring devices that are not sufficiently granular in scale, and that therefore cannot collect data on much less than a solar scale, means it is highly unlikely that human beings will ever be able observe manifestations of the non-human civilisations that exist out there, actually way out there, within the vastness of intergalactic space.

By asserting this we answer the question and affirm that, yes, there are certainly non-human beings and civilisations existing throughout the physical universe. The universe is too vast, and the creative and evolutionary impulses embedded in everything that exists are too powerful, for there not be billions of species existing throughout the physical universe.

However, we note that there are even more species, billions upon billions more, that are not limited to a purely physical existence. Some of these have traditionally been called spiritual beings, but it is more correct to say that all the species and identities in existence are energetic beings. The physical, if identities manifest physically at all, is just one part of their overall existence. This is a significant point, and it indicates why scientists on this planet will always have difficulty observing traces of non-human beings. They not only have a restricted perspective, being able to observe only from the surface of this planet, but they also narrow their view to the physical. This is an even greater limitation.

The universe can be likened to an iceberg. You well know that most of an iceberg's mass exists under water, out of view of those on the surface. Similarly with the universe, only the tip of its physical manifestation is apparent to observers on this planet. The vast major proportion of the universe is not seen by scientists who limit their data gathering to physically measurable effects.

To put this another way, species exist within particular energetic bandwidths. All the organic species on this planet—being carbon-based life-forms that draw on a similar base of DNA and genetic code—exist on the same energetic bandwidth. So when they bump into each other, they bounce away—or one grabs the other and eats it. They can interact in this manner because they exist on the same energetic bandwidth. Similarly, when you put your hand on a tabletop your hand stops there, your hand doesn't travel through the tabletop. This is because your hand and the table share the same bandwidth. However, not all species throughout the universe share the same bandwidths. In fact, you, as a human being, exist on more than just one bandwidth. You partake of several. This leads us to make a number of observations relevant to the question.

First, it is most definitely the case that other beings throughout the universe exist on energetic bandwidths that significantly differ from the human physical bandwidth. As result, scientists on this planet will never be able to measure their presence. The bandwidths involved are so distant from the human that they do not intersect.

Another relevant factor is that many species are able to shift across bandwidths with great facility. This means that, just as is depicted in science fiction literature, some species that in general exist on a non-human energetic bandwidth are able to manifest on a physical bandwidth, should they choose to do so, and become visible to human beings. We observe that those you call extra-terrestrials may be considered to fall into this category.

How is it possible for some species to traverse bandwidths with ease? The human species, homo sapiens sapiens, is considered to have existed for 200,000 years. We won't comment here on the DNA configurations that sustain biological life on this planet, including the human, except to say that they date back eons before the Earth came into existence. At a mere 200,000 years the human species has existed for only what could be considered a blink of the cosmic eye. Additionally, the scientific revolution began just four hundred years ago, and the technological revolution less than two hundred years ago. In contrast, other species in the universe have existed for millions of years. It is easily understood that they have developed capacities that are unimaginable to human beings. Or, at least, to mainstream scientists and thinkers. Science fiction writers and their readers are considerably more open-minded and so capable of appreciating that non-human species operate in ways that differ considerably from what is considered to be the basic human experience.

This brings us to comment on human experience. This experience is actually broader, and encompasses more bandwidths, than is usually given serious consideration. To offer one example, there are times when a human being's hand can move through a tabletop. This is possible because human beings have what may be called an energy body that exists side-by-side with, or, more exactly, is superimposed over, their physical body. When a person detaches their awareness from their physical body and attaches it to their energetic body they may observe their energetic hand pass through a physical table. There is also a phenomenon called lucid dreaming, in which individuals experience aspects of reality that are immediate and vivid in a way that appears to echo physical reality, but that are not physical. In such instances people are using their energetic body to experience an energetic component of reality that exists in close parallel to physical reality. While in their energetic body they are able to pass their hand through a table, walk through walls, and fly across a city. Out of body experiences and near death experiences, in which people look down and see their injured body, also involve the energetic body. While praying or meditating people may also connect their everyday awareness to their energetic body and travel into non-physical bandwidths of reality.

So we are proposing that the human form has both physical and energetic components. The energetic component of the physical body includes electricity that sparks neurons in the brain and stimulates hormones that carry information from one part of the body to another. Beyond this there is, as we said, the energetic body that is a counterpart to the physical body. The physical body itself consists of a narrow bandwidth of the total energetic bandwidths that are available to human beings. All this still doesn't include the spiritual component of human identity, which functions on yet another bandwidth.

Currently, humanity as a species knows little about these various bandwidths. With the exception of a few dedicated explorers, they understand even less how to utilise them. One upshot of learning how to use their non-physical bandwidths is that doing so facilitates communication with other species. We are referring here to meditators and psychics who make contact with beings existing on non-physical bandwidths. We note that many who ingest psychedelics, particularly in shamanistic activities, are also able to access non-human identities. They can do so because they are connecting to the non-physical bandwidths that are naturally part of their human awareness. On the other hand, there are many beings who exist on bandwidths so far beyond the human that they will never be accessed. Just like human scientists who will never be able to fully map the universe from this tiny planet existing on the outer arms of a small galaxy far from the centre of the universe, so there are many aspects of reality that just cannot be observed from the human bandwidths.

To complete our answer, we wish to bring the discussion back down to earth, specifically to discuss a non-human species that has been on this planet for eons. No, we are not referring to what are popularly known as extra-terrestrials. Rather, we are referring to elementals. These are energetic beings who associate with natural places, such as mountains, volcanoes, large forests or small woods. Another variety of non-human beings associate with plant and insect species. In ancient times these beings were variously called nature spirits, sprites, elves and fairies, and those who could communicate with them were known as shamans and medicine men and women. In later times, especially in Christian lands, those who had knowledge of elementals were labelled witches and wizards and punished.

There is much misunderstanding regarding elementals and their capabilities. Many eons ago human beings worshipped local elementals, even offering them sacrifices in appeasement so they wouldn't cause harm. This was an error. Elementals largely exist in parallel to human endeavours. They certainly do not exist in a causative relationship. That is, elementals do not interfere with human activities, nor do they intercede on any individual's behalf. Their focus is on whatever place or species with which they associate. Notice we say *associate* and not *inhabit*. Most elementals associate with a physical place. Or, to be more exact, they associate with the natural processes and species that co-exist in a physical place. That physical place may be small or quite extensive. One elemental may associate with an entire island, while another focuses on just one small area within that island. Elementals naturally engage with different levels of energetic and physical activities in whichever places they associate. So elementals themselves may be said to exist on different energetic bandwidths.

If you wish, you may make contact with elementals. This needs to be done respectfully and with a non-aggressive, curious intent. Anyone attempting to make contact seeking personal power or wanting to control an elemental will not have much success. In fact, going into anything with a negative intent will give rise to responses you may not enjoy. Not that elementals are dangerous. It's just to warn you that you inevitably get back what you send out.

Another class of non-physical beings inhabit pets. Most people know perfectly well that their pet dog, cat or horse has its own personality. What they may not be as clear about is that the pet that looks back at them has a spiritual being on the other side of those eyes. Your relationship with your pet is a relationship between spiritual equals. Different certainly, because each exists at a slightly different bandwidth. But their and your bandwidths sufficiently overlap that you are able to interact. We note that this capacity for communication has evolved over the millennia. To take the example of dogs, back in Paleolithic times wild wolves started approaching human beings. This approach was initiated because the wolves were hungry and the human beings had food. The human beings shared their food and gradually, over time, the wild wolves adapted into domesticated dogs. Puppies and children were trained to appreciate one another, and in this way humans and dogs formed an inter-species communication link. That link is now fixed, which results in the beings inhabiting human bodies and the beings inhabiting dog bodies being naturally tuned into one another, making interaction straightforward. A similar link exists with other species, particularly horses who are highly sensitive to human interaction.

Most other species lack such a direct link. You could, if you wished, communicate with the elemental associated with a beehive, or a meadow, and learn from them what the hive or meadow needs in order to function at its highest level. Elementals associated with a mountain range or volcano have likely been there for eons, so they potentially have much to share, having observed and experienced much. But their level of functioning is very different to the human. This is because their energetic bandwidth is much further removed from the human bandwidth compared to the spiritual identities present in dog and horse species. With less bandwidth overlap there is less ability to communicate and share. Nonetheless, some overlap exists, making a degree of sharing possible.

We offer this information because what people too often miss is what is happening around them. It isn't necessary to look away from this planet to find non-human beings. There are many are right here beside you, existing in parallel to your daily existence.

Question 5

Who, or what, am I really?

You say human beings occupy certain energetic bandwidths. So what are we? Are we glowing energy? Are we souls trapped in bodies? Are we angels? Are we extraterrestrials? Are we spirits? Who, or what, I am really?

THE GUIDES RESPOND:

Over the millennia human beings have described their spiritual identity in many ways. These descriptions were offered in the context of the cultures in which they lived, using concepts then current and creating metaphors that reflected their way of life. This is as it must be. However, humanity today is living in a very different culture to what their forebears did. As a result, concepts regarding the nature of reality are radically different. Accordingly, it is appropriate that in response to this question we offer ideas and metaphors regarding human identity suited to these times.

We begin by commenting on our preference for the word *identity* when describing what has historically been known as the human soul. At your core you are a spiritual identity. Identities possess a number of fundamental facilities. One is volition. You can choose or not choose to do certain things. Another is the ability to accumulate: as you act on your choices you accumulate experience. Another is growth. As you accumulate experiences you learn from them, which feeds your growth. You, as a spiritual identity, will then incrementally evolve into something greater than you are. As befits identity, you possess unique qualities. The make-up of your undeveloped core is unique to you. As you gain experience, learn and grow, what your core identity evolves into continues to be unique to you. The sole reason you have incarnated on this planet is because it provides you with an environment in which to experience, learn and grow. So this is why we call you an identity. You are not just a soul that is what it is. You are an identity who is continuously learning, accumulating, evolving.

Naturally, you have a spiritual existence that is separate from, and independent of, your physical existence. So to answer one part of the question, no, you are not trapped in a body. You have willingly entered it and embraced it. We say this while acknowledging that you may often wish this was not the case. Life, as we all know, is often overwhelmingly difficult. Yet as *Ecclesiastes* observes, there is a season for everything. While you are embodied it is a season for struggle. When this embodied state ends other seasons follow, offering other kinds of experiences and other varieties of learning, which are usually less onerous and less demanding of you. In the meantime, you are living inside a body and asking: who, or what, am I? The question is asked because no answer is obvious to those who ask it. It is likely you are asking because the old religious answers, that you are a soul, or possess Buddha nature, or are a spirit, are too vague to be satisfactory. Accordingly, we will provide some detail regarding what you are.

Central to the mystery of being human is the relationship between your physical body and your spiritual identity. This is more straightforward than is usually stated, but also more complex due to the layers involved. To describe this relationship we will draw on the conceptual demarcation previously made between the electrophysical, the electromagnetic and the electrospiritual. These are the three primary bandwidths within which human beings function.

Your body exists on the electrophysical level. Your body can be described as a biological system that combines matter, chemicals and electricity. Information circulates around your body via electrical charges that pass between nerve endings. These nerve endings include the synapses in your brain. Information-carrying electrical charges initiate chemical reactions that motor your body as you go about your day. Some of the information is apparent to you at the level of your everyday awareness, such as when you read a newspaper or respond to another person's voice. However, most information circulating through your body is not immediately apparent to you, given there are many biological processes, such as the digestive process of extracting nutrients from food, in which your conscious mind does not need to participate. This is your identity on the electrophysical level.

Associated with your body is an electromagnetic spectrum. The closest to your body is what has historically been called the aura, for which we prefer the term energetic envelope. The energetic envelope has two major functions. It provides an energetic template that guides the growth of cells when an egg in a woman's womb is fertilised. It also provides an energetic medium for the passing of information from the spiritual to the embodied levels of existence. Another significant aspect of the energetic envelope is that it incorporates energy centres known as chakras, as well as the meridians along which focused energy moves around the body—although technically such energy doesn't pass through the body, it circulates through the energetic envelope, along the meridians and via the appropriate energy centres. It is through the energy centres that a spiritual identity associates with a body and is linked to what it experiences. This, then, is the part of your electromagnetic system that is associated with your body. It came into existence when the egg and sperm first formed a zygote that rapidly grew into your physical body, and it will dissolve after your body dies. Those who wish to learn about this in greater detail are directed to read *The Kosmic Web*.

Other parts of the electromagnetic system are closer to the electrospiritual aspect of your identity. These include the traits we have described elsewhere as your accumulated human identity. These traits are characteristics you generate during the course of living an embodied existence, and that you carry with you from one life to another. They are characteristics that contribute to your unique identity. They don't dissolve when your body dies, being uploaded to and energetically inscribed into your electrospiritual identity.

Your electrospiritual identity may be thought of as a sphere of glowing energy. Just as different individuals' energetic envelopes possess different colours, and just as your energetic envelope changes colour to reflect your inner states, so electrospiritual identities possess different colours, which may more accurately be termed different energetic signatures. While each individual's core energetic signature remains the same always, much can be and is added to it as an individual evolves. More can be said about this, but it will have to be another time.

To return to answering the question, it can be said that at your current stage of evolution—a stage you share with every other person who is on living this planet or is waiting to be reborn into another human body—you possess two basic types of identity. When you are embodied your identity incorporates the electrophysical, the electromagnetic and the electrospiritual, with the first dominating your awareness, the second supporting it, and the third present to your awareness to varying degrees, depending on how much you actively seek to engage it. It should be noted that most of what people consider to be psychic activity, along with what people call spiritual experience, involves utilising the electromagnetic capacities associated with the human body.

The second basic type of identity occurs when you are in a non-embodied state. Then your electrospiritual identity dominates your awareness, although the way it expresses itself is modulated by the electromagnetic characteristics that adhere to it. By this we mean that if you believe something intensely during your life on Earth, this will modulate what you experience in a non-embodied state. Perception is a complex process that simple categorising cannot come close to describing. What we have just said about the non-embodied state is cursory in the extreme, but we hesitate to say more because to do so we would have to use terms and metaphors that relate to embodied human existence. And a consequence of our doing that would be that you would receive an impression that the spiritual realm echoes the human realm, just on a grander scale. This would be a false impression.

The fact is that the relationship between human spiritual identity and human physical identity is much more complex than we have just implied through our demarcation of your identity into the three levels of electrophysical, electromagnetic and electrospiritual. A hint of this complexity may be seen by examining the belief that aspects of the human world echo what is in the spiritual realm.

In one sense the human world *is* a dim echo of the spiritual realm, given your spiritual identity's awareness has to be reduced so it can associate with your human level identity. Accordingly, what you experience within the constricting limits of your limbic and cognitive systems, the emotions you feel and the thoughts you have, echo at a lesser level what you feel and think when you are not embodied. So human love may be considered to be a lesser echo of agape, spiritual love, and human thinking is a much reduced process compared to the expansive thought in which you engage on the electrospiritual level.

Nonetheless, it is precisely this constriction that is so useful for developing your potential as a spiritual identity. Getting into difficult situations, then having to work your way out of them again, feeds your evolution as a spiritual identity. Without embodiment, without subjecting yourself to the tough and marvellous situations human existence offers, your identity would accumulate experiences much more slowly and without the nuances that being human offers.

Of course, there are other worlds you could incarnate into, other cultures you could experience, and other kinds of learning to be had. One possible experience that is notably different to what you are experiencing on this planet is being part of what is termed a hive mind. Submerging independent awareness into a hive activity, which includes merging feelings, thoughts and volition, is an experience that would appeal to some human beings but be repugnant to many more. In fact, as a context for experiencing, learning and growing, being part of a hive mind has its own strengths, limitations and inherent difficulties that identities have to struggle with before they are able to fruitfully function within it on an adult level.

The point we are making is that in order to experience embodiment you don't need to come to this planet. There are literally billions of other physical worlds, which function according to very different physical, cultural and energetic norms than the human. There are also worlds that function entirely on the electromagnetic level. It is possible to enter many of these worlds in order to challenge yourself, develop your abilities, learn, and evolve.

The hive mind culture to which we just referred is represented in human culture as alien, as involving extraterrestrials. The question was asked, are you an extraterrestrial? We answered this previously in the positive, given that all electrospiritual identities that occupy human bodies on this planet originated via an entirely spiritual process that occurred far from the Earth. As a result you have had to migrate from an electrospiritual place—we mean "place" metaphorically, not literally—to reach this planet. Therefore it may be said that, yes, you are an extraterrestrial.

Are you also an angel? Our answer is yes and no, depending on how you define an angel. If you consider an angel to be a non-physical identity which has higher capacities, including agape, insight and wisdom, we would say yes, you have the potential to become angelic. On the other hand, if you associate angels with spiritual identity, then everyone is an angel, in which case the term loses its coherence, because angel then is not separate from the human. In that case, you may as well drop the term angel and just use the term of human spiritual identity. If you consider an angel to be a messenger from God, then no, you are not an angel. And neither is any other spiritual identity who visits you, whether in your dreams, during prayer or meditation, or while you are going about your everyday life. The notion of angels as divine messengers is simply incorrect. As we stated in a prior answer, God as creator is too far beyond the human world to interface with it, so it certainly doesn't send messages via couriers, angelic or otherwise. Reality functions in other ways, as we are attempting to clarify in all our responses.

For the reasons we have just given, we prefer not to use the word angel. It has religious connotations that we wish to avoid when discussing spiritual matters. Besides, even in a religious context the concept of angel is deficient. Religious art depicts angels as possessing glowing bodies and wings. By now it will be clear that spiritual identities don't have bodies, and they certainly do not need wings to shift between the different layers of reality. The fact is that spiritual identities come in many sizes, shapes and capacities, and possess what, from the human perspective, is an infinite variety of energetic signatures. This makes them much more nuanced and interesting than the bland, generic term of angel allows. This is another example of the human tendency to shrink down what is expansive and nuanced to their own limited and simplistic perspective. It offers yet another reason not to use the term angel.

Much more has and will be said about your nature as a spiritual identity. Some statements you can confirm while embodied, others will only be fully understood after your body has died. We know that some readers will struggle to assimilate what we say, while others will read the same words and a light bulb will switch on in their minds. For some our words will act as a pathway into what they now consider mysterious, pointing a direction to explore. For others our words will serve as reminders, helping them recall what they already know. For such seekers, our words will open a pathway between their human self and their spiritual self, which in turn will allow information to trickle down to them that they accumulated in previous lives.

What opens you up to deep information is self-enquiry. By enquiring into your existence, and especially by enquiring into the specifics of who, what, where and why you are the way you are, you become able to penetrate into the mystery of your identity. In the process you learn what for you is new. You also become able to draw down from your spiritual self what you have previously learned, which then enables you to normalise it within your current life.

It is through self-enquiry that you can learn the principal features of your life plan and the goals you have set yourself. You can discern the obstacles preventing you from achieving your goals, and appreciate how they came into existence. This includes grappling with formative experiences that occurred during this life, in childhood, as well as with those you underwent in previous lives and that are now impacting on your current life. Through self-enquiry you may also learn to recognise ingrained patterns of feeling, thinking and behaviour, which will provide you with the information you need to combat those that are limiting you and to nurture those that aid your growth. Self-enquiry will give you the tools you need to delve into the mystery that is your own spiritual nature.

For this reason we recommend self-enquiry as a most useful aid to your spiritual development. If you wish to delve into the mystery of who and what you are, self-enquiry will help you do so. And it will also have the sought-after consequence of bringing you closer to your bliss. Accordingly, we recommend self-enquiry as a tool that could benefit you on many levels.

Question 6

What does
self-enquiry involve?

I'm aware of two types of self-enquiry. One is the philosophic approach of Socrates, the Greek philosopher who had people question the values and assumptions they lived by. The second is that of the Indian sage Ramana Maharshi, who advocated looking beyond the superficial aspects of identity to focus on our spiritual self. The first looked at how we live in the world, the second sought the part of us that transcends the world. Which approach do you advocate? What does your form of self-enquiry involve?

THE GUIDES RESPOND:

These are certainly two forms of self-enquiry. There are others. Jungian analysis offers a means for people to understand their deep drives that otherwise function at an unconscious level. Spiritual traditions such as Buddhism, Kabbalah and Indian meditation each have their own methods of self-enquiry that help people understand their identity and why they act as they do.

Each method was developed within a particular culture and so was appropriate to that culture. In that sense, none is better than any other. However, we observe that the psychological analysis of human behaviour is more nuanced today than in times past. Concepts and practices developed within depth psychology have opened up to scrutiny a great deal of previously unknown impulses and psychological traits that are present in the human psyche. Notions such as projection, co-dependence and erotic fixation were certainly not canvassed in earlier eras. One reason is that in the past self-enquiry was carried out within closed groups and within relatively rigid religious outlooks. The possibility available in the twenty-first century—on the back of the wide-spread dissemination of psychological insights, which enables self-enquiry to be unshackled from religious beliefs—means a wide range of concepts and practices are available to whoever wishes to delve into what makes them personally tick.

The one proviso we add to this last sentence is that while we advocate unshackling self-enquiry from long-standing religious beliefs, nonetheless we consider your spiritual nature to be central to self-enquiry. This is because you are a spiritual being. Accordingly, drilling into your identity so far that you uncover the spiritual roots of who you are is certainly, as Ramana Maharshi proposed, a necessary part of self-enquiry. So is the Socratic approach of examining the values and attitudes you live by. You need to confront all the assumptions you rely on, because inevitably some will not reflect reality. All this is fundamental to self-enquiry as we envisage it. It is fundamental to practising a method of self-enquiry appropriate to these times. And it is basic for those who wish to understand the deep basis of their existence.

Do we advocate for a particular form of self-enquiry? We do. However, before we discuss what this entails, we need to state clearly that our recommendation is not the only form of self-enquiry that is valid for today's enquirers. Nor is it necessarily the form that is best suited for you, the reader who has, we assume, approached this book seeking clarification regarding how best to understand the subtleties of your existence.

Many things come into play when you choose a form of spiritual practice to help you develop your potential—or we are perhaps better to say *forms* of spiritual practice, because often people change their practices as they progress through a life. This is especially so today, when lifetimes do not end after just two or three decades, as was the norm in the past. As in everything else in life, you must make your own choice of spiritual practice, based on what you consider to be right for you, which you decide after listening deep inside yourself.

Pragmatism is a key concept here. It is up to you to choose a form of self-enquiry based on what works best for you. You then need to stick to it. Consistency of practice over an extended period is crucial to making progress in any discipline. On the other hand, being able to move on when one practice has been thoroughly explored is also an important skill. Many factors contribute to individuals remaining attached to a form of spiritual practice long after it has ceased to deliver what it initially did for them. Such factors, and the inertia they give rise to, are themselves useful targets for self-enquiry. Eventually, everything you feel, think, say and do must be questioned. All traits have their strengths and weaknesses, a period when they are useful and a time when they cease to be so. All this must be understood.

Given this answer is being provided in the month of January, the notion of New Year's resolutions is relevant here. However, instead of merely replacing an unwanted character trait with another you see as more beneficial, which is what New Year resolutions usually involve, we suggest you expand the notion to include an annual review of your life, in which you honestly list problem areas in your work and family life, then use that list to impartially confront your shortcomings. All practices of self-enquiry need raw data to work with. Self-observation provides the raw data. And an annual review will undeniably provide you with plenty of data. Of course, you don't need to wait until the next New Year to carry out a review of your life. As is humorously said, now is good!

So the accumulation of data is fundamental to self-enquiry. Beginning this task by listing problems in your life is straight forward because, given no one is perfect, problems are always present. The key driver of your personal life problems is that you have contributed to them, either by initiating an activity that has led to another individual flaring up at you, or circumstances in your life have made you sufficiently uncomfortable that you yourself have flared up at someone else. Alternatively, instead of involving other people, it may be your life circumstances that are the problem, that you have a difficulty you are unable to resolve. Whatever is the case, the point is that you need to examine what in you has contributed to the problem forming.

Once you have identified key issues in your life, and gathered relevant observations regarding your role in creating them, many different forms of self-enquiry are available for you to use in addressing them. We are about to describe one such method. We do not propose that you automatically abandon a practice that already works for you and adopt the approach we are about to advocate. Pragmaticism is essential. If you find a particular practice is useful, keep doing it. Alternatively, if it has lost its usefulness, move on to something else. The important issue is that you keep progressing. And progress occurs as a result of choosing a practice that works, committing to it, and carrying it out over an extended period of time.

We will now address the question, what form of self-enquiry do we advocate? Self-enquiry needs data to consider. Data is obtained via self-observation. Observations take two main forms. The first consists of observations of your behaviour. This includes what you say in reaction to others' actions. In particular, note your repeated behaviours, along with the words and phrases you repeatedly use. The second form is internal. It involves observing your thoughts and feelings.

Successful self-observation requires you not to defend or justify yourself, as this will colour your observations. You need to learn to separate from yourself sufficiently to observe what you think, say, feel and do. This involves learning detachment, so you are able to examine yourself like you would another person for whom you have no strong feelings. Learn to enter a dispassionate space inside you from which you can observe yourself as you go about your life. This in itself is a skill that is learned only gradually.

Practising meditation and learning how to disrupt, then silence, the constant flow of thoughts that pass through your mind will help. What is required is the development of a quiet, observing self inside you. Ancient Indian meditators called this the witness. Meditation can help you find the witness within. Once you have found this part of you in a quiet state you can then practise centering your attention inside it during the hurley burley of everyday life. This is difficult, but is one way to sustain a state of self-observation.

We acknowledge that what we have just described is a skill developed by an accomplished spiritual practitioner. When you start out it is likely you will not be able to consistently achieve this detached witnessing state. Accordingly, we recommend you begin by making occasional observations of whatever stands out during your daily interactions. Especially pertinent are moments of anger, frustration, subservience, or of any other reactions you have to life situations, that afterwards, when you think about them, cause you to inwardly cringe. Make a note of such instances. We recommend you keep a journal to record your observations. Another strategy is to identify an ongoing problem in your life and note all details of your behaviour, feelings and thoughts in relation to that problem. Dreams are also worth recording, as your deep mind often releases important observations into your everyday mind via dreams.

Now that you have a store of accumulating data, you can start sifting through it. Patterns will become obvious. In certain situations, involving the same person or persons, it will become clear, if it isn't already, that you feel, think, say and do the same things. What you have done is identify a pattern of behaviour. Psychologically, patterns of behaviour are grounded in character traits.

Having collected a store of observations, and having discerned repeated patterns in them, the next stage of self-enquiry is analysis.

How do you analyse behavioural patterns? How do you identify what character trait or traits are involved? Here you need a framework. As we have said, many valid frameworks apply. The framework we recommend, and are developing in tandem with our scribe, draws on the psychological framework presented via the channelled Michael Teachings. The virtue of this framework is that it is reincarnational in approach. It situates life plans at the centre of its analysis, and its terminology is entirely psychological in nature, being devoid of religious notions such as sinfulness or that God personally directs individual lives. Many published books present the Michael Teachings materials. We have also presented our own interpretation of the Michael psychological framework in our *Channelled Spirituality Series*. For those who desire more detail, those books are recommended.

However, if you already have a preferred analytical framework, there is no need to change from it. The purpose at this stage of self-enquiry is to identify the character traits that generate behavioural patterns, so use concepts and terminology that work for you.

Once behavioural patterns and their associated psychological character traits are identified, the next step is to track them back to formative circumstances. The first step in tracking is to examine your childhood, because it is usually at that time of your life that you formed the key character traits that continue to shape your personality. These key traits are directly linked to the coping behaviours you adopted to help you deal with the particular circumstances you faced during childhood. Some traits formed during childhood are positive and provide a sound platform for growth, others are negative and limit your growth. Fear underlies all coping behaviours. We have discussed this elsewhere, along with how specific self-limiting traits develop out of particular varieties of fear.

Beyond your formative childhood years, some key character traits will be grounded in what happened during a previous life, which has given rise to patterns of behaviour that you are working through now. In addition, karmic connections may also be involved in the way a character trait plays out in your current life. If you negatively and significantly impacted on another person, and are now working things out between you, this will require you to confront and resolve the traits that led you to transgress on the other person's freedom in the first place. In general, you'll be able to recognise if formative events are located in a previous life because nothing in the childhood of your current life appears to be sufficiently powerful to give rise to what is a dominant way of feeling, thinking or doing.

Note, however, that often you choose a childhood in which a key formative event echoes what occurred in a previous life. This is so the same patterns of feeling and thought will be triggered this time round, which makes it easier to work on them, easier in the sense that they are so centre stage in your life you can't avoid them.

This brings us to the issue of your life plan. A significant portion of your life plan is designed to help you develop your strengths and confront your limitations. The point is, you have selected whatever is included in your current life's plan, just as in earlier lives you choose to focus on developing certain of your strengths and reinforced particular weaknesses. People commonly say that no one escapes God's judgement. The real truth is that you cannot escape the consequences of your own decisions. Sometimes decisions are made on the spur of the moment, at other times they are made after deep consideration. Whether spontaneous or considered, all your decisions have an impact on the contours of your life and on the lives of other people. Those impacts echo through lifetimes. Negative impacts only cease to have an impact when they are addressed.

We have discussed negative and limiting psychological traits at some length here. Positive traits are also fostered in each life. Often people discount these because their negative traits loom so large. Sometimes other people may talk up your positive qualities to get you to feel better about yourself. This can be a useful temporary pick-up.

However, ultimately—and here we adopt the dispassionate outlook we discussed earlier—it is most useful to be realistic when you examine your life and to balance positive with negative qualities. By this we mean, seek equally to recognise whatever is enhancing your growth and whatever else is limiting it.

This, then, is an outline of what we mean by self-enquiry:

- Self-enquiry begins with making observations, a practice that requires a degree of inner detachment.
- Second, accumulate observational data, either remembering observations or recording them in a journal.
- Third, analyse the data, sifting it to discern repeated patterns of behaviour.
- Fourth, identify formative situations and events that stimulated the formation of those repeated patterns of behaviour. Start by looking at your childhood. If there appears to be no key event or situation in your childhood, look back further. Meditation can help with this process, as can asking your deep mind for an informative dream before you go to sleep.
- Fifth, once you have completed the analysis, formulate a way to overcome negative traits and the self-limiting patterns of behaviour they give rise to.

In this way, self-enquiry provides a means for you to confront your psychological limitations and to initiate self-transformation.

Question 7

What is the best way
to practise self-enquiry?

I appreciate what you are saying about self-enquiry. But what do you recommend I do to practise it? Am I better off enquiring on my own, or should I join a group? If the latter, what sort of group? And what if there isn't any group nearby? What should I do?

THE GUIDES RESPOND:

We always advocate being pragmatic. Do whatever works for you in your current circumstances. For some people this means working in groups, for others alone. However, we have a number of observations pertinent to each approach.

One of the primary benefits of working in a group is that it involves setting a regular time when participants meet. Meeting once a week is traditional for metaphysical and self-study groups in recent times. This is arguably optimal, because it focuses participants' attention on their immediate issues on a regular basis. Life is always busy, so establishing a regular meeting time clears a space in everyone's weekly schedule, providing an opportunity for deep engagement. However, do whatever is practical and possible. If biweekly or even once a month meetings are all group participants can commit to, then do that. The important outcome is that meetings are held regularly and that meetings be continued for an extended period of time. We leave it to each to decide how long is appropriate.

If you are engaged in solo self-study, we recommend you similarly set aside a regular time to "meet up with yourself". This will ensure you maintain momentum. It is easy for a week or two to pass without any inner progress being made. As we keep saying, sustained, regularly repeated effort leads to progress. It is more effective in the long run, by which we mean in the run of your life, than short bursts of intense and energetic commitment, which are followed by fallow periods in which you do little.

The second observation we would make about groups is that they can degenerate into social interaction or follow-the-leader. Neither scenario is optimal for advancement. Many people attend groups for their social opportunities. This is understandable and, in ordinary circumstances, to be commended, given so many people feel disconnected in today's world. Group activities that connect people to others who share their interests, and more importantly their deep passions, promote the well-being of all involved.

However, when spiritual groups become primarily opportunities to interact socially with others, their deep value is blunted. The reason spiritual groups exist is to provide an opportunity for participants to connect to their spiritual self. If social interactions come to dominate the group's activities, then everyone's socialised self is primarily being engaged, not their spiritual self. This situation is not conducive to personal growth.

With regard to what we have called follow-the-leader, everyone goes through periods in their reincarnation cycle when it is beneficial to them to follow the instructions of a teacher or guru. Conversely, everyone also undertakes the experience of leading others, whether in a spiritual group or in some other context, most commonly work or war—which is not to condone warring, just to comment on what commonly occurs in the human domain.

Anyone who incorporates a leadership role into their life plan does so because it provides an opportunity to develop their skills. They also have weaknesses that they are using the leadership role to address. What this means is that leaders are not infallible. They are not all-knowing, and they are certainly not manifestations of the divine, however that notion is formulated.

Followers often want their teacher or guru to be some kind of super-person. They tell themselves and all who will listen that they are following a great teacher or an important sage. In part, they do so because this makes them feel they are special, that they are in the privileged and rare situation of associating with a spiritual giant. This is actually another example of the socialised self interfering in the optimal activities of a spiritual group. In this case, the worshipping followers are compensating for their own frustrations and limitations. They are projecting their personal desire to be wise onto another individual. Psychologically, they are allowing hurt existing at the level of their socialised self to divert their focus from engagement with their spiritual self. All projections must be understood to involve deflections from engagement with your own deep identity. Certainly respect those who are more experienced and knowledgeable than you, but do not excessively revere them or think they are your spiritual superior. They are not. It is almost certain that this super-person will not always manifest the wisdom that followers project onto them. Sustaining an image of a great and wise guru usually also involves followers turning a blind eye to their teacher's weaknesses. All this is unhelpful to group members' spiritual progress.

You will go through periods of following another person. This is understandable. Everyone needs a teacher, even several teachers, who they can look up to and model themselves on during the course of their life. But when the following extends for years, even for decades, then psychological traits such as dependency and feelings of unworthiness need to be acknowledged.

The best teachers are those who are able to help their students develop their own potential. Teacher-student relationships are most effective when they are focused on sharing particular skill sets or learning particular lessons. When the skills are developed, and the lessons learned, it is usually appropriate for those involved to go their separate ways.

Another aspect of teacher-student and guru-follower relationships worth commenting on is that they are based on human ideas of social hierarchy. The teacher is usually considered to be superior to the student. Similarly, the guru is viewed as spiritually higher, often very much higher, than followers. While teachers certainly possess skills that their students are learning, the assumption that a guru is necessarily spiritually superior to followers is incorrect.

In terms of skills, students often show themselves as being more talented than their teachers. This applies in all fields: music, sports, horticulture, and so on. So the differences between teachers and students do not result from the teacher being superior but are due to experience and opportunity. While mutual respect is always to be condoned, no one is intrinsically higher or lower than another. It is more accurate to observe that each is at a different stage in their cycles of learning and growth.

In the case of one person being markedly more able than those around them, that results from them having worked on developing their skills for more lifetimes. Once others work on the same skills for a similar number of lives, they will develop their own expertise in that field. Both having expertise, neither will be better than the other. Differences between them will exist only because each expresses their expertise in ways that are personal to them.

Similarly, it is never the case that the guru is spiritually superior to followers. This is another situation in which people inappropriately project ideas of social hierarchy. We have two comments specifically about this kind of judgement—and it is judgement, because any time people say one person is superior it necessarily involves adjudging others as inferior.

Our first comment is that there is no hierarchy on the spiritual level. Everyone is unique. And everyone is equal. Certainly, some spiritual identities are more experienced than others. But this doesn't make them superior. It just leads to them having more to share. And those they share with will one day be as experienced as they are, and will in turn pass on what they learn to those who are inexperienced.

Our second comment is that it may be that a follower is actually more spiritually experienced than their guru. The individual who has adopted the role of follower may be working through psychological traits that require them to be in a socially subservient situation. Alternatively, they may be inwardly unbalanced, in the sense that their socially-formed self is dominating their personality, resulting in their experienced spiritual self being buried under their overly active socially oriented drives. Or it may be that the follower has taken on that role to learn humility or to serve others. There are many possible explanations for why a more spiritually experienced individual would be the follower of a less spiritually experienced individual. What this means is that socially constructed notions of hierarchy that people project onto others, elevating a few above the many, are incorrect. Such assumptions do not reflect how, at a deep level, things actually are.

Accordingly, we recommend a non-hierarchical structure in a self-enquiry group. Certainly, there is a need for leadership, because some are always more experienced, more driven, and more desirous to take up a leadership role. But no leader or teacher is spiritually higher than anyone else. They are just in a better position to share. As we noted earlier, mutual respect is best for promoting everyone's growth. No one is superior or inferior. Everyone is merely at different stages in their growth cycle.

This leads us to a consideration of what group-centred self-enquiry is best suited for: the sharing of experience. Bringing to the group what you have learned, and thereby pooling knowledge, is to everyone's benefit. You also learn through the exercise of articulating what you have learned. And you will learn from what others have learned. When self-knowledge is shared in a group, in an environment in which participants respect one another, much genuine progress can be made.

It is due to the opportunity to pool knowledge that group self-enquiry is more effective than going solo. On the other hand, going solo means you don't have to deal with the grating of personalities that are inevitably part of group interactions. In addition, as the saying goes, there is a season and time for everything. Sometimes during your life you are better off drawing inspiration in a group setting. At other times following your own course is more appropriate.

To return to the question, which asked whether solo or group work is better, we suggest you weigh it up. Ask yourself, what is best for you now? You are the person who is in the best position to answer that question.

As for what group to join, that is also a matter of personal assessment. If it helps your decision-making, draw on others' advice. Articulating to another person what you are looking for is often sufficient to help you clarify to yourself what is best.

Clearly, it is unlikely a group that teaches our exact approach to self-enquiry is available, at least not at the time this is being written. So find a group that most closely approximates our recommended approach. Alternatively, set up a group of your own. A group only needs two or three attendees. Even one other person can help you focus your efforts and sustain your momentum over the months and years necessary for serious progress to occur.

Question 8

What form should a self-enquiry group take?

Do you have any suggestions for what form a self-enquiry group should take? Is it necessary to have a formal structure? Or should those participating do what suits them? What do you recommend?

THE GUIDES RESPOND:

In answering this question we wish to offer some recommendations without being proscriptive. So what we are about to say is best seen as possibilities, not necessities. We adhere throughout to the view that you are the one who is living your life, you have to deal with the consequences of whatever you choose to do, so our intention here is to offer suggestions. Select from our response whatever suits you. Or reject all we say and follow your own course. Ultimately, you will follow whatever course appeals to you anyway—which is entirely appropriate and to your benefit.

We begin by observing that people join spiritual groups because they feel a lack deep within. This feeling emanates from their spiritual self. It is important that the feeling not be deflected into the socialised level of your self, by which we mean that you not respond to a feeling of deep lack by increasing your social engagement, such as taking up a new hobby or seeking a new relationship. The feeling that something significant is missing deep inside you is, in effect, a gift to you from your spiritual self. Use the energy it provides as intended. This, then, is our first observation: Use the energy provided by your feelings of deep dissatisfaction to enquire into the who, what and where of your existence.

Naturally, this precludes allowing the feeling of lack to drag you into depression. Unfortunately, depression often goes hand-in-hand with feelings of deep dissatisfaction. Depression in turn involves a series of related feelings, such as feeling trapped, feeling that things are hopeless, feeling that nothing can be done. These are self-limiting emotions that result in stasis. Accordingly, while we are proposing that a strong feeling of lack is a positive emotion which makes energy available to you to initiate a fundamental change in your life, there is no benefit if that energy is drained into the stagnant pool of depression in which you wallow feeling trapped and hopeless. You are not trapped, and your life is certainly not hopeless.

Most things in human existence have a double-edge. This results in emotions typically having an upside and a downside. The upside of feeling your life lacks something significant is that it provides energy, which comes from your spiritual self and that you can use to alter the course of your life. The downside is that some of that energy leaks into what we call your gloopy self. This is the part of your psyche, a kind of black hole, around which self-defensive coping behaviours circle. Your gloopy self has its own inertia, which acts to keep you stuck mentally and emotionally. That some of the energy generated in you by your spiritual self will leak into your gloopy self is inevitable. The energy has to flow somewhere. Paradoxically, if you do not use the energy to initiate change, it will feed your feeling of being stuck and unhappy.

Elsewhere we have discussed that you have two fundamental momentums in your life. One momentum is that of your life plan. The other is provided by your gloopy self. When you feel a deep lack, it is your spiritual self calling you to change track and get into sync with your life plan. Alternatively, when you ignore your spiritual self's call, psychologically you divert the spiritual self's energy into your gloopy self and reinforce its momentum. This is the double-edge in play. It is intrinsic to human existence. It is what makes human existence such an excellent testing ground.

The result of this is that when you are in the process of selecting a spiritual group to join, what you fundamentally need the group to do is help you sustain a shift in momentum so you can enact your life plan. Sometimes this will result in you feeling that a particular group is right for you. The feeling of rightness is deep because it exists at a pre-mental level. That is, it doesn't involve logical thinking. In such a case, the feeling that the group is the right place for you to be comes from your spiritual self. However, there is a danger here. The danger is the feeling of rightness may also come from a more superficial level, from your unstable emotions and from your socialised self. This is another example of the double-edge.

We would like to say that if you have doubts about a group you approach, then this is not the group for you. Alternatively, if you feel certain, if you have no doubts, then this is indeed a group worth joining. However, we warn you that the opposite may in fact be the case. Sometimes when people first attend a group meeting they are unsure whether what is on offer is right for them, but over time, and after consistently practising what is taught, they discover that in fact the group works for them. Alternatively, what initially feels right may come to feel not right. These things happen. How, then, should you decide? That is over to you. What we will say is that if you feel stuck in your life, it is better to try something new than not do anything at all. And whatever happens, whether things work out with you and the group or not, you'll learn something valuable about yourself.

The important thing is that *you* choose. Don't allow others to persuade you one way or the other. Listen deep inside yourself, without thinking, without drifting on a tide of intense emotion. Become quiet inside, and open yourself up to the gentle guidance of your spiritual self. It will let you know what course is best.

As regards what a self-enquiry group should include in its meetings, we have no specific recommendations. However, we do suggest two things are essential. The first concerns mental reorientation.

One of the fundamental changes that people engaging in a spiritual quest need to make is with respect to their mindset, to how they look at the world. In ordinary terms, this is your world view. Religions offer believers a set view of the world. This includes a history, a list of significant individuals—usually identified as saints and sages—and a metaphysical prescription for unhappiness that includes ideas about your deep self, the basic spiritual choices human beings face, and what happens after your body dies. Religious world views provide a mix of truth and fantasy, the latter accumulating over time as religious leaders add their own interpretations of what has been proscribed before, and because incorrect ideas are reinforced by those who don't perceive the real relationship between the spiritual and physical domains.

Generally, when people first join a spiritual group they need to reorient their world view to get into sync with what is on offer. Of course, what is on offer may itself contain errors. This is inevitable because of how human beings function. Nonetheless, if the group offers concepts that shake individuals out of a more limited outlook, then that is beneficial to them.

As a general statement, what is most beneficial is changing your outlook from a religious to a spiritual view. By this we mean shifting from a metaphysical perspective that involves ideas like good, evil, salvation, election, condemnation, ascension, and heaven and hell, to an empirical spiritual perspective based on direct experience of the spiritual domain. Elsewhere we have identified the religious perspective as top-down and the spiritual perspective as bottom-up. The bottom-up view is grounded in personal experience, and derives metaphysical statements from experience. That is the approach we recommend.

Otherwise metaphysical statements consist of handed-down dogmas. Metaphysical statements that are validated by people's experience are to be preferred. Of course, when you begin exploring the spiritual domain many metaphysical statements, including those we are offering, will refer to things beyond your personal experience. As such, they are speculative. These are best regarded as possibilities, not certainties. As you develop you will be able to test speculative statements to discover for yourself whether or not they are correct. If you find they are, then metaphysical speculations become valid for you, in the context of your life experience.

Accordingly, we suggest that meetings include metaphysical material that draws on people's experiences. This applies whether participants draw on their own experiences, on other people's published accounts, or, what perhaps is optimal, a combination of both. Metaphysical theorising is most effective if it is bottom-up and derived from experience, as opposed to a top-down approach, which transposes long-existing religious beliefs onto your experiences. In this regard we refer to common statements such as, "God did such-and-such to you", or "This is what sacred texts say about what happened, so this is how you should interpret it." Our view is that using long-standing religious beliefs to contextualise personal experiences does not promote the development of your understanding.

To summarise. A group committed to fostering self-enquiry is best to include material that helps reorient each participant's mindset to a metaphysical perspective that is empirically grounded and free of ready-made religious formulations. We have presented suitable material through our scribe, and will continue to generate more. A great deal of other suitable material is also available, some channelled from a variety of non-embodied sources, and some written by insightful individuals inspired by their higher self and beyond.

The second requirement we consider essential to a successfully functioning self-enquiry group is that it has a psychological framework that helps participants understand their psychological make-up. Establishing a shared framework has several purposes. It enables all group participants to use the same terminology. Misunderstandings arise when people use words others don't understand, or when they use the same words but don't appreciate that they are each giving those words different meanings. A common vocabulary, with agreed definitions, is essential to fruitful discussions of deep matters.

Another result of having a shared psychological framework is that everyone can contextualise their perceptions in the same way. Earlier we observed that an advantage of joining a self-study group, as opposed to going solo, is that everyone can pool their experiences. A shared psychological framework also aids analysis by putting everyone on the same page, so they are using the same terms and ideas when sharing from themselves. Our books, under the title of the *Channelled Spirituality Series*, provides a suitable psychological framework. But as we stated earlier, self-enquiry groups around the world use many different frameworks, and very successfully.

The third point we wish to make about analytical frameworks is that they need to be nuanced. Human psychology is complex. Psychological frameworks need to accommodate this. A framework also needs to acknowledge factors that result from reincarnation. Such factors include taking into account the ways that life plans contribute to each individual's psychological make-up, what skills they are focusing on this time round, and what key obstacles they face. This is the minimum a psychological framework needs to acknowledge and address if you want to get down to the nitty-gritty of who you are and why you are where you are.

These are our recommendations concerning what a self-enquiry group requires to enable participants to progress. However, we are also aware that successful groups tend to evolve by a process of trial and error. Participants try something, then adjust it until they discover what collectively works for them. This applies to the format meetings could follow.

Our scribe's training occurred within a group that drew primarily on G.I. Gurdjieff's Fourth Way teaching and utilised a process of self-enquiry similar to what we have been describing here. The group's metaphysical material was largely drawn from the Sufis, the Gnostics and Buddhism. Meetings began with a brief meditation, which was followed by a reading and discussion of a spiritual text. The meeting then progressed to psychological analysis, which was spurred by one participant each week reporting on their self-observations and progress. This is as good a format as any. Alternative formats could involve participants focusing on a particular psychological trait during the week, as a form of homework, and reporting back on what they found, or using a spontaneous format, in which whoever has a significant issue puts it forward for group discussion and analysis. Smaller groups tend to have more flexibility with their format than larger groups. As we said, the format group participants find most useful to them can be established through trial and error.

Our final comment on groups is that participants easily become convinced that their group, and its understanding of spirituality, is the best. This is an example of how easily and naturally the gloopy self insinuates itself into a process that is intended to involve the highest spiritual motives. Be on guard against such unnecessary self-congratulatory attitudes.

How does psychological analysis clarify my life plan?

Your advice on group formats is very straightforward and reasonable. However, I'm struggling to understand how investigating my psychological make-up helps me understand what my life plan is. What's the rationale?

THE GUIDES RESPOND:

This question takes us to the heart of why we are recommending a process of self-enquiry. Earlier we made reference to the veil that hides the deep intent that has initiated your life this time round. The veil may be characterised as consisting of the circumstances of your daily existence. All the things that occupy you day-to-day—all your hassles, enjoyments, relationship problems and satisfactions, family matters, work matters, thoughts that keep circling the same issues, feelings and desires that won't go away—these constitute the stuff of your daily existence as a human being. They are also the veil that hides the deeper aspects of your existence from you. This is because when your attention is fixed wholly on them you are unable to see deeper into your life.

It might be thought that we are characterising the activities of your daily existence as shallow compared to spiritual intents. This is not so. All you experience during daily life is significant. It is what you signed up to embrace when you decided to begin an extended cycle of incarnation in human form. It is what provides the opportunity for you to hone your awareness, to learn new skills, and to grow through exploring opportunities and overcoming obstacles. In no way are we slighting daily human existence by suggesting it is shallow or of little consequence. We repeat, it most certainly is not.

On the other hand, we *are* recommending that you view the stuff of your daily existence in another way. That is, look hard at it and try to discern the patterns within it. The metaphor of a veil conjures the image of a cloth that hangs before your eyes. It suggests that all you need do to perceive the spiritual depths is lift the veil. But before you can lift the veil you need to know what the veil is. This returns us to the notion of pattern, for the veil has an intricate pattern woven through it. This pattern is unique to you. In fact, each and every person has their own specific veil, featuring a pattern that is theirs and theirs alone. How so?

Earlier we drew attention to the fact that you have a life plan. Each individual, before they are born, selects the key features of their upcoming life. These include the characteristics of the body they will occupy, the family they will be born into, the culture they will grow up in, the key problems they will grapple with, the significant decisions they will make, the individuals—family, friends, antagonists—who will help and challenge their decision-making, and so on. Once you are born and begin following the course of your life, you begin engaging with or declining to participate in the opportunities you organised prior to birth. You make decisions on the fly, acting on inner impulses, deflecting impulses into related activities, or ignoring them altogether. You also act spontaneously in response to desires, on whims, because you want to please others, or to get at them.

These factors form an intricate, multi-leveled pattern made up of psychological traits, emotional and physical behaviour, and a predisposition to repeatedly embrace certain possibilities and avoid others. Collectively, these factors form a behavioural and psychological pattern that is unique to you. It could be called your personal veil. The chief characteristic of a veil is that it hides something. So when you lift the veil what is hidden will be revealed. In the case of your personal veil, it is not so much a matter of lifting it as of making it transparent. That is, we are recommending you transform your personal veil from an opaque cloth into an information-rich vehicle of insight that illuminates for you what is motivating you in this life. You do this by closely examining your veil's pattern.

In industrial circles researchers regularly use a process called reverse engineering. This occurs when one country downs another country's more advanced military aircraft, or when a competitor steals another company's prototype. Technicians then examine the piece of hardware and analyse it to discern not just how it was physically manufactured, but to understand the combinations of scientific principles that were utilised to construct it and make it operative. This is the same process we are advocating here: that you, in effect, reverse engineer your current life to understand the deeper factors that led to your current talents, weaknesses, behaviours and character traits being present within you. You do so by examining the circumstances of your life and analysing them to discern what led to you being the person you are, living in the circumstances you are, making the decisions you are.

A question could validly be asked here. Most spiritual seekers have been told that by lifting the veil, by looking beyond the physical and social aspects of their existence, they perceive the deeper spiritual reality that underpins all existence. Yet we are saying something else. We are saying that what you discern are psychological traits, and these are certainly already present in everyday life. So where is the spiritual mystery we promised earlier? Where is the deep penetrating insight into the truly profound aspects of existence?

This is an important question. We raise it because answering it provides another significant insight into the nature of your life.

First, you are at all times a spiritual identity. At any moment you can lift your awareness out of the circumstances of your daily existence to perceive reality in entirely spiritual terms. At least, that is a possibility. Yet it is a possibility not many people take it up. Indeed, few people know they can step beyond their everyday human self and embrace their non-embodied spiritual identity. Many deny such an identity exists, while others believe they can only engage with it after their body dies. And even among those who accept they are a non-embodied identity, few possess the skills to regularly engage with it. Why not? What is the difficulty? The difficulty is that most people are intensely engaged in what they incarnated to do: they are engrossed in the complexities of their everyday existence.

Human existence is demanding. All the people you interact with, all the circumstances you face—from simple to tricky, from mundane to profound—require your close attention and so grab most of your daily energy. The demanding nature of human existence makes it very difficult for you to shift your attention to the veil, let alone look beyond the veil and perceive the deeper reality that underpins your physical existence. What is required is that you gather your energy and use it to energise your attention so it may be lifted out of a state of being constantly caught up in everyday existence. And you can only do that by learning what is holding your attention within everyday existence. In other words, before you can engage with deep spiritual reality you need to study and understand all the factors that "glue" your awareness to life circumstances.

Accordingly, in order to develop spiritual insight you need to dismantle what is tying you down and preventing you from attending to deeper matters. This is why we recommend self-enquiry. It provides a practical way to spiritualise your daily life. It enables you to unshackle your awareness so you are no longer wholly caught up in the minutiae of human existence. It helps you to broaden your perspective and deepen your insights.

We make a final observation to conclude these comments on the process of self-enquiry. While you are fundamentally a spiritual being, during the course of incarnation you enter a human body and so become immersed in the physical, social and psychological aspects of human existence. You do this repeatedly, life after life. In the process you build up a store of skills and traits. You also develop abilities and talents and nurture whatever in human experience attracts you, both positive and negative, freeing and limiting. Progressively, one small step at a time, everyone matures. As result, the factors you select as part of your life plan in each life do not exist in a void, by chance, or as one-offs. Each life plan builds on what went before. This means that the pattern on your personal veil is not arbitrary. You put it there. Furthermore, by examining the pattern closely, by identifying what factors are present in your personality and life circumstances, you can "reverse engineer" your own life and come to understand what exactly has led to you being who you are, and doing what you are where you are. In this way you can come to appreciate your own deep identity, why you are drawn to certain people and situations, why certain situations are holding you back and stopping you from achieving all you wish to, and what you need to resolve in order to keep progressing.

Your incarnation cycle on this planet involves a process of maturing, by which you gradually become an experienced, skilful, loving, knowledgeable individual who others perceive as wise. The process of self-enquiry, which helps you foster your strengths and identify and eliminate your weaknesses, is an extremely useful addition to your toolbox of skills that facilitate your self-transformation.

Question 10

Isn't it easier to ask a medium or hypnotherapist?

That sounds like hard work! Why can't we just take a shortcut and consult a medium about what our issues are, or get a hypnotherapist to dig the relevant information out of our mind? Isn't that a much more straightforward option? It would also be so much easier that what you're advocating!

THE GUIDES RESPOND:

This is a very reasonable question. Today's world is full of labour-saving technologies, devices you use to wash your dishes and clothes, vaccuum your floors, clean your teeth, build houses and wash cars. They save much time, energy and effort. Hypnotherapy and mediumship are technologies that also save time, energy and effort for those seeking to understand what is going on in their life. If these technologies can help you, why not use them? They seem to offer a pragmatic way to address mysterious matters that are otherwise difficult for people to get their minds around. We acknowledge all this. Nonetheless, our view is that there are occasions when a jack hammer is appropriate, and other times when you are best being hands-on and using a simple spade. In what follows we will discuss why.

When people first start enquiring into their selves, the one over-riding factor everyone encounters is that they can't see deeply into their psyche. We used the metaphor of a veil in our earlier answers to illustrate this lack of perception. But even if you ignore the veil by closing your eyes, what do you see? It's so dark in there you don't see anything at all!

Elsewhere we have used the metaphor of a cave to describe how, deep within your psyche, there are the equivalents of caverns, trails, streams and rivers. Much fear arises in relation to this, because people imagine that strange creatures scuttle through the cave, giant spiders perhaps, or boogymen, seductive sirens, murderous monsters, and the beasts that haunt your nightmares. This is all the result of projected fear. The fact is that if you entered the cave of your psyche, the only strange creature you would meet is you. Or, at least, aspects of you. These aspects are both pleasant and unpleasant in nature. Where they perhaps startle is that they may be more intense than those you encounter in everyday life.

Sigmund Freud theorised that human beings have an id, a well of subconscious urges. These urges are only prevented from bubbling up and acting very rudely by the ego. The ego is the inhibiting part of the psyche. It is shaped by social norms, which teach individuals from a young age to conform to society's rules. So dinner guests' disagreeable urges to argue or throw another guest across the room are suppressed by the ego. When the id is suppressed by the ego, acceptable dinner party behaviour results.

We acknowledge that Freud's theories about the particular parts of the subconscious are widely rejected today. Nonetheless, his general concept holds true: you have urges buried deep in your psyche that are disturbing at the everyday level. Some of these urges came into existence during your childhood, when you perhaps suffered physical or emotional trauma. Others are buried even deeper. They originally arose in response to what happened to you in prior lives. Some urges manifest especially intensely because they go back to what happened to you in a past life as well as during this life. When you become aware of these aspects of your psyche they are unsettling, even profoundly disturbing. If you saw how you have responded to demanding situations in previous lives you would think that parts of you were monstrous. We don't mean by this that you were a psychopath or murderer, although that is possible. We just mean that the intensity of your past responses would demolish your sense of yourself as being a reasonable, balanced, socialised person.

The point we are making is that people's fearful feelings that scary things exist deep in the dark cave within is true insofar as there *are* aspects of their psyche that would seriously scare them if they met them face to face. From this we conclude that the reason people fear going into their psyche is due to the knee-trembling terror of meeting not monsters foreign to them, but themselves.

When a child is scared to do something, an adult takes the child by the hand and leads him or her into the scary situation and shows the child that it isn't so scary after all. Similarly, when people seek to know deep things about themselves, they often seek out someone who not only can hold their hand, but who can walk into the darkness ahead of them. This is the function of the hypnotherapist and the medium. They use the technologies they have mastered to enter the caverns within and tell a troubled enquirer what is there. As with everything else in life, there are pluses and minuses in asking someone else to enter your psyche on your behalf.

The first point to consider is that the psychic expert necessarily filters through their own mind whatever information they glean. Each psychic expert also necessarily possesses certain strengths and weaknesses. They are often better at perceiving some aspects of the psyche, while other aspects they don't have much of a feel for at all. Their personal experience plays a role in this. So does their training.

The second point to consider is that some psychics and hypnotherapists are open to allowing non-embodied identities to contribute to the process of opening up the enquiring individual's psyche. Non-embodied identities usually have deeper perception and greater access to information than the therapist or medium. How much of what non-embodied identities know gets through to the enquirer depends on how open and how perceptive the psychic experts are.

In addition, if the non-embodied identity is a member of the enquiring individual's circle of guides and teachers, then the identity's knowledge of the individual enables it to direct the session towards what is most useful for the enquirer. The flow of information on that level again depends on the psychic expert's openness and skill.

A third issue to consider is that questions asked by a troubled enquirer are often too general to elicit really useful information, or are even beside the point. This is a fundamental issue. If you approach a medium or hypnotherapist, they are guided by what you wish to know. If you are missing the point regarding what is happening to you in your life, then you get much less out of the process than you could. To be fair to hypnotherapists and mediums, many are able to look behind an enquirer's questions and see more deeply into what is involved. But then there's the issue of the enquirer not seeking information of that depth, and so not being intellectually or emotionally prepared to receive it. As a result the session isn't effective. We'll illustrate this point with an example.

Let's say a mother is grief-stricken at the death of her daughter. So she goes to a medium seeking assurance that her daughter is fine. Her feelings are actually mixed. She wants to know her daughter exists contentedly in the afterlife. But she also knows there were failures in their relationship. So she wants to know that she is forgiven—although she might not be able to consciously articulate this. She is also suppressing the realisation that she wasn't as good a mother as she could have been. Her spiritual self knows this, and has been telling her. That's why, in part, she has consulted the medium in the first place. She is responding to her spiritual self's promptings. But once she is with the medium she asks the wrong questions, or, at least, she doesn't ask the questions that could lead her into the darker parts of her self where the problematic attitudes and emotions that disrupted her relationship with her daughter lie. So from the session with the medium she gets the reassurance she seeks that her daughter is fine, and to that extent she assuages some of her guilt. But she doesn't get any closer to understanding what really went on between her and her daughter, let alone uncovering enough knowledge of her own limiting traits to start working on them.

This is why we say there are times when a spade applied by hand is more useful than a jack hammer. In order to get the most out of labour-saving technology, which is what hypnotherapists and mediums provide, you first need to do the spadework. Then, when you're very clear about what has to be done, you can bring in technology and achieve much in a short space of time. But you don't start with the technology. You do the spadework first. We'll explain.

When you enquire into what lies behind your life, when you wish to learn about the deep motives that drive you, or when you seek to uncover what is behind a trauma that is making you unhappy, the most effective approach is to grapple with it yourself. You're the person who is best placed to do that, because it's your life and your identity that you're enquiring into. As the saying goes, you're Johnny on the spot. To return to our cave metaphor, when you wish to enter the dark and somewhat scary cave of your own psyche, there's no point sending someone else in on your behalf because then you don't undergo the experience. You don't feel the nuances, you don't learn all there is to learn from the process of exploring. On your wedding day you don't send in a surrogate to marry your beloved on your behalf. Similarly, there's no point sending another person into your psyche to dig things up for you. It's a job you need to do yourself.

In order to be effective when exploring within you need some kind of map to indicate the general features of the human psyche. And you need a pragmatic process to identify features that are particular to you. We have provided both a map and a process in the books of *The Channelled Spirituality Series*. Assistance will also be offered to those who wish to initiate their own process of self-enquiry via courses that are not yet available at the time of writing this response, but will be in the future.

The purpose of self-enquiry is to gradually increase your understanding of your deep nature, both psychologically and spiritually. No one is able to understand everything in one hit. The human mind is incapable of processing all the information involved, and no human personality is robust enough to handle it if all the information did become available. From the perspective of everyday life, weird stuff is involved. And scary stuff. Even frightening stuff. Why frightening? Because reality is so much more complex and layered, and there is so much more going on, than your everyday awareness is able to access. The only way to cope with uncovering it without being overwhelmed is step by step.

Elsewhere we have said that information is given to people on a need-to-know basis. You are told things as you need to know them in order to get through difficult times, process life lessons, or digest puzzling events. Who chooses when it is appropriate for you to be told something new? You do. You do it by enquiring into the nature of your existence and by puzzling over what you don't understand. Sometimes it takes years of puzzling, years of chipping away at an question. But when you really need to know something, eventually the information is uncovered. Furthermore, because you will have worked through a number of issues related to what you are enquiring into, and because you have gradually acclimatized your everyday identity to what is involved, when you finally access the information you will not be bowled off your feet, you will not be emotionally knocked flat.

To return to the metaphor of the spade, let's say you have a situation that drainpipes and cables are buried in the front yard, but no one knows exactly where they are. As a first option you don't send in a mechanical digger. That's not appropriate. First you use a spade and dig by hand to find where the drainpipes and cables are. Let's say they're buried quite deep. As you dig down you need to ensure the hole doesn't collapse on top of you. If the soil is crumbly, you give the hole's sides a slope, or if the hole's sides are vertical you put up wooden boards to prevent collapse. Similarly, as you dig inside yourself, doing so carefully, step by step, enables you to take care of your psyche, to uncover and process each new aspect one at a time. This ensures you don't collapse psychologically.

Only after you have uncovered the buried pipes and cables, and identified the direction in which they run, do you bring in the mechanical digger. Now you can be confident that the digger won't damage anything it shouldn't and that its work will be effective. Similarly, after you have identified drivers deep inside your psyche, and you know what they are, how they have impacted on you, and especially after you have learned to insulate yourself from their emotional impact, only then is it appropriate to go to a hypnotist or medium and ask them to help you get some rapid, effective digging done. It will be effective because you know precisely where you want them to dig. And you have the questions that go deep and to the heart of what is involved. At this stage you know what you need to know. And you will assuredly be given what you need.

Who does the giving? We have discussed this in another book in this series, *Where Do I Go When I Meditate?* There are a number of possible sources for information. The most common is your own spiritual self. If you need to know what happened during your childhood, or in a past life, it can tell you. It knows because it was there. Other questions may be answered by your soul friends, or by your non-embodied guides, or, more rarely, by someone beyond.

We conclude this response by noting that whatever you learn is driven by your own questioning. Many people flounder in their self-questioning. They know things aren't right in their life, but either through fear, or because they don't have an effective process of asking, they don't make much progress. In the book *Experimental Spirituality* we spent some time discussing how to ask effective questions. Those who wish to know more about how to ask questions that uncover useful insights are advised to go there.

This question began with the observation that the process of self-enquiry sounds like hard work. It is. The questioner then wondered about taking a shortcut to self-knowledge. Unfortunately, there is no shortcut. And pursuing one will leave you short-changed.

However, it is possible to progress more quickly or more slowly. That is completely over to you. So while digging with a spade can be slow and hard going, the sooner you roll up your sleeves and get into it, the sooner you'll be able to get the digger in and make rapid and significant progress. Self transformation involves periods of hard grind and rushes of deep insight.

We wish you well as you seek to learn more about who you are.

Why are some spiritually gifted while the rest of us aren't?

Why do some people end up being mediums or channellers? Are they special in some way? Are they privileged? I guess what I'm asking about is how some people have a direct connection to the spiritual and the rest of us don't. Some are gifted, most aren't. Why this difference?

THE GUIDES RESPOND:

It is the case in human life that little is as it seems to be. We begin answering this question by observing that this principle applies here.

When people look at another person who possesses something they don't have, or can do things they can't, they effectively raise that person to a higher level while simultaneously lowering themselves. For some this is accompanied by an emotion of envy regarding what are viewed as the other person's gifts. Or it may be accompanied by a feeling of personal inadequacy, or worse, given individuals can become very negative towards their own life situation and abilities compared to what that another person has. That people have such a feeling is understandable. As the saying goes, it is all too human. Nonetheless, it misses the nuances of what is involved.

First what appear, to others looking on from the outside, to be great abilities or gifts are often not experienced that way by the individual who possesses them. Reading the biographies of famous people who achieved much will quickly reveal the extent to which many such people were haunted by their own feelings of inadequacy or loss. Some utilised their ability to make up for something they or someone else in their family did—it is wise not to underestimate the extent to which the single-minded application of talents or abilities is part of the human psychological compensating mechanism. Such people can live their life having achieved great things, and been publicly applauded for it, but on their deathbed still feel that they hadn't accomplished what they could or should have. Issues that arose in prior lives are likely involved in such feelings. So this is one instance in which people looking from the outside see another as being privileged, but the person doesn't feel that way about themselves at all.

Alternatively, many people feel that their supposed gift or privileged life situation is a burden. Often this is because deep inside they have a nagging feeling that something isn't right, that they need to do something particular, but they can't put their finger on what it is. They may then choose something in their life and engage with it, developing it to high level. It may be their work, or their children, or a hobby they obsess over, or something else. Again this is a variety of compensatory behaviour, filling their attention so they don't have to address the hole that lies deep within. Such people can be driven and accomplish much, and so earn great money, accolades or social status, yet the nagging feeling that something in their life isn't quite right never goes away. It is there, deep inside them, waiting to bubble up in times of quiet, stress or self-doubt.

We are speaking generally here in order to situate the question into the wider context of human psychology. Our point is that despite appearances, no matter how smooth, seductive or even glitzy someone else's life appears, under the surface there are always undercurrents. Always. And these undercurrents make the life situation of any person perceived to be privileged other than straightforward.

We have commented on feelings of inadequacy or deep pain that the talented and successful can have, which drives them to achieve more in their life than is usual for human beings. Other situations involve an individual deliberately taking on an ability in their life this time round and expressing it to a high degree. We will now examine this scenario, expressly in relation to individuals who become mediums or channels, and consider the extent to which they may be privileged. Or not.

There is a saying that nothing comes for free. When people say this they are usually thinking there is a cost to what someone gets, that a privileged person is getting a free ride now but there will be a price to pay later. Often this saying is offered without knowledge of the life situation of the person being talked about, and particularly without knowledge of how that person came by what appears to be something that was freely given to them. We observe that envy often lies behind such claims, or, alternatively, the feeling that life is unfair, which itself derives from the claimant's sense of inferiority. Our position is that in reality nothing is given freely. If one person has what others do not it has been earned. And there is not so much a cost involved, or a price to pay, as a responsibility to be discharged. We will explain what we mean by all this in relation to mediums.

Mediums perceive or sense things that others don't. Their perceptions result from being able to function like a window. We mean this in the sense that just as light passes through a window from outside and into a room, or alternatively passes from an illuminated room via the window into the outside world, so the medium's awareness functions as a window via which information passes into them from beyond, or passes from them into what exists beyond the physical. The difference is that where a window conveys light, a medium conveys information. What sort of information? This is where different forms of mediumship come into play.

Some mediums can communicate with the deceased, for example by passing information between living and deceased family members who remain concerned about one another. This is one of the most common forms of mediumship. It has certainly been practised for a long time. But other forms of mediumship are just as common. For example, clairvoyance, when a person receives information about an event in advance of it occurring. Or spiritual healing, when a medium facilitates the passing of healing energy to a sick person from an external spiritual source. Or telepathy or intuitive insight, when a person receives a thought or emotional impression that arrives via perceptions that are not sense-based and that informs them of something they didn't previously know.

Telepathy and intuitive insights are experienced by almost everyone at some time in their life, apparently accidentally and unplanned, and so are a surprise when they occur. While they are experienced as eruptions into everyday physical awareness, they are actually experienced energetically, via the aura. Telepathy, in which you become aware of what another is thinking, involves information being exchanged via two people's energetic envelopes, which functions as the medium via which information is shared. This is a skill that is developed and so is present in many people's accumulated human identity. Intuitively received information could come from many sources: from another person's awareness, from your own store of experience, from your spiritual self, or from further afield.

Because during the evolution of the human species on this planet both telepathy and intuition helped people survive, they are skills everyone has. That they are not used on an everyday basis is because few people are taught about them. While mainstream culture accepts their existence, as is depicted, albeit somewhat sensationally, in the superhero movies that are currently so popular, scientists ignore or deny their existence, while others, including many religious believers, are fearful of them. This has created a situation in which the arrival of information telepathically or intuitively creates head-scratching among those who receive them or those who choose to study them.

Nonetheless, not only do they exist, but, as we just noted, at some time during their lives everyone experiences them. However, right now we are not discussing instances of unplanned mediumship, but when mediumship is deliberately utilised.

To discuss this we will focus on the situation of the medium who can convey information between the living and the deceased. Incidentally, elsewhere we have called the deceased the extra-living. This is because they, of course, are not dead at all, given the spiritual identity who once occupied a now dead body continues to exist after their body has ceased to do so. We name them the extra-living because those in the non-embodied state have extra capabilities compared to those in the more restricted embodied state.

First, let us assert that a medium who is able to pass information between the living and the extra-living is not practising their abilities by accident. They have planned to do so. This is also the case when people, who have had no prior exposure to mediumship, start spontaneously, and often surprisingly to them, being able to communicate with the extra-living. Utilising such abilities is always part of their life plan. If people are uncomfortable with these abilities, wonder if they are imagining their extra-perceptions, are filled with doubts regarding whether what they are doing is for good or ill, or if they are very comfortable with their ability and exercise it whenever they can—all these feelings of puzzlement, unease and comfort are part of their pre-life plan to work with that ability during this life.

What has to be remembered is that such abilities are not a one-off occurrence. Each of you is living through an extended sequence of around one thousand lives. During all these lives you explore numerous possibilities available in the embodied state in general and specifically in the human domain. Human existence fundamentally involves learning about the connections and overlaps between the physical, the psychological, the practical, the emotional, the intellectual and the spiritual aspects of your existence. You incarnate repeatedly because no one is an expert the first time they attempt to do something. Becoming accomplished takes practice. Whatever you wish to do, whatever you get good at, and whatever mistakes you make on the way through that then need to be rectified—it all requires repeated incarnations. Talents develop out of abilities that are worked on life after life, until eventually they become an embedded skill set that the individual is able to creatively apply at will.

That it would take multiple lifetimes to achieve a level of expertise is straightforward. Where things get complicated is that talents don't come in a bubble, separated from everything else in your psyche. Talents are just one part of your overall identity. And no one develops expertise in all parts of their identity equally, to the same level and at the same time. So a person may become highly capable as a medium, freely and easily passing messages between the living and the extra-living, but in other parts of their psyche they will not have anywhere near that same high level of skill and confidence. Moreover, those aspects in which they are less able will likely seep into their activities as a medium and impact negatively on it. We need to be more specific to convey what we mean.

Let's say a person is functioning as a medium, helping those who have lost family members to reconnect with them. As the medium becomes well known more people seek them out, so the demands on their time and energy increases. How will they cope with this? Will the demands become too great? Will they come to regret having this skill? Or will they become full of themselves, lapping up the attention? Will they experience a crisis of faith, wondering if this is what God really wants them to do? Will they become competitive, wanting to be the best known medium? Will they become snooty, deciding they will only work with a certain class of people? Will they help everyone without distinction? Or will they seek to become the medium of choice for important and well-to-do people?

These types of psychological issues go hand-in-hand with any talent people develop then manifest with any degree of expertise in their life. Such issues must not be thought of as being a negative. Nor should they be characterised as the cost of being talented, or as the price the talented must play. We actually view these kinds of psychological issues in the opposite light: the medium's talent offers an opportunity to positively express a skill in which they have developed expertise, while simultaneously working through other related aspects of their psyche that don't function at the same high level.

In order to understand how this works, how people choose, as part of their life plan, to work with both positive and limiting traits, we have introduced the concept of accumulated human identity. As you live life after life you acquire skills, develop innate abilities, and nurture talents. You also acquire habits, some useful, which aid your skill-building, others negative, which hold you back. We refer in particular to self-destructive tendencies and traits that unbalance your psyche, such as envy, jealousy, greed, addictions, self-pity, and so on. When your body dies everything you develop during the course of that just-lived life, positive and negative, nurturing and debilitating, self-enhancing and self-limiting, gets uploaded to your spiritual identity. Those traits, habits, skills and abilities then contribute to the growth of your accumulated human identity.

This means that whenever you plan a life, you have your own experiential store to draw on. So anyone who is functioning as a medium in this life is drawing on abilities they have developed over a sequence of lives, which they have chosen to express this time round. They do not have to do so. In their next life they may not show any skill as a medium at all. They may even be sceptical that such skills are real. Whether they draw on or decline to draw on anything present in their accumulated human identity depends entirely on what they have decided to work on during an upcoming life.

Each person's life plan incorporates working with and nurturing positive qualities, such as skills, abilities and talents, and working to transform negative and limiting traits into those that are positive and so help them achieve their goals. Pre-life planning involves organising situations to make this work possible. In the case of our hypothetical medium, this means that the spiritual identity has planned a life in which they intend to positively utilise their talent to help others, while also working on negative traits that arise in conjunction with their talent. For example, the medium may be born into a family in which many other family members are psychic, so the medium's talent is accepted and nurtured from childhood. Alternatively, the future medium may choose to be born into a family in which psychic abilities are ignored, are considered a fantasy, or condemned as the devil's work. In these cases non-supportive or restrictive childhood input will have been selected to highlight negativities and issues the individual had previously struggled with. So this situation would provide the future medium with something to work against, ensuring they have to make considerable effort to overcome instilled negative feelings and doubt in the process of working to make their ability blossom. To speak generally, what family environment you are born into depends on what exactly you have planned for yourself this time round. In the case of our hypothetical medium, a specific family environment is selected that offers the best fit for the related positive and negative qualities she or he wishes to work on.

So, and to answer the question, when it appears that some people are psychically or spiritually gifted where others aren't, it is not that these people are special. They're not. A medium who chooses to express their skill in this life may not do so in their next life. Similarly, if you feel you display no such natural talents, it is not necessarily that you don't have them, or haven't exercised them in a previous life. It is just that you are currently focused on other things that don't involve mediumistic skills. You at the level of your spiritual self know this very well, but you at the level of your human self do not. You at the level of your gloopy self may even feel left out, may feel that life isn't fair, that you should be sharing in the action that others are getting, that you should be having the same fun others are enjoying. The fact is that you are working through your own life plan, and mediumship isn't part of it right now. And besides, as we just noted, the medium's life is never all lightness and fun. They will be working through their own darker issues that you likely don't see.

This leads us to the issue of working with abilities responsibly. Responsibility is an unavoidable part of adult human life. Being a parent involves taking on the responsibility of having children. The fact that not everyone is automatically nurturing as a parent makes being a parent a skill that has to be learned. People often experience trauma during their own childhood, which subsequently impacts on their behaviour as a parent, either by modelling a parental role to them that they subsequently adopt, or by providing a scenario they choose to work against to ensure that as parents they don't traumatise their own children in the ways they were traumatised themselves.

As a general statement it may be said that traumatic childhood situations are selected pre-life. This is not always the case, but it does occur so often that it may be accepted as a rule of thumb. The reason experiencing childhood trauma is selected—whether it involves a single high intensity event, or lower level events that build over time—is so that negative traits present in an individual's accumulated human identity may be brought into the life to be worked on. The aim is that by confronting them they will eventually be overcome and eradicated. Mothers and fathers not doing to their children what was done to them is one facet of learning to act responsibly as a parent.

Many other roles similarly involve exercising responsibility. Being a teacher, nurse, social worker, politician, manager, journalist, truck driver, gardener or boss involves being responsible for and to others, as well as being responsible for and to oneself. Our hypothetical medium has a responsibility to the living and extra-living people they are connecting. Responsibility involves providing them with the service they desire as well as exercising discretion and sound judgement, given it is sometimes better if a client who is driven by the gloopy part of their self is not given all the information the medium is able to access. Acting responsibly is another skill that is developed over time, as you experience a wide range of circumstances, and as you learn from the mistakes you inevitably make. At this point we will discuss responsibility specifically in relation to channelling.

Becoming a channeller is an ability that is selected pre-life. This makes it part of the channeller's life plan. All that we have said about using the opportunity to bring out associated negative traits while developing an ability responsibly applies to channelling.

Channelling is a subset of mediumship. To speak broadly, there are two types of channelling. The first is when the channeller is open to all kinds of input. Channellers who practice automatic writing, deliberately opening up their awareness to information passed on by any spiritual identity who comes by, is an example of this first kind of channelling. Mediums who connect the living and the extra-living are opening their awareness up to others and channelling the information they receive. The second type of channelling is when the channel passes on information from a very limited number of identities. Our scribe is an example of this type. Let us make clear there is no hierarchy between these two types. One is not better or more advanced than the other. They are just different ways of acting as a medium. Having clarified this, we will discuss responsibility in relation to this second type of channelling, using our scribe as our example.

Many people from a young age are possessed of a drive to accomplish something specific. For some this manifests in a sporting ability. For others it becomes visible in a facility for music, art, writing, or in play, such as when a child acts out nursing and doctoring scenarios, or enjoys organising other children. Many people naturally manifest their deep abilities in this way. But some among these young people feel a drive inside themselves to accomplish something above and beyond their ability. They don't usually know what this is. They may experience an inner drive that suggests a purpose or even a mission, but for a long time they can't pinpoint what this purpose or mission is. This was the case with our scribe. The drive he felt to accomplish something specific was a major aspect of his life plan. We refer, of course, to the plan to work with non-embodied identities to share information on the human situation and how it might best be negotiated.

But just having this feeling of being driven didn't mean he would automatically perform his part to put this plan into action. Preparation was required. This preparation may best be described as involving a series of steps. He had to negotiate his way through childhood, then his teenage years. He needed to respond to his spiritual self's push to examine life—his own life specifically, and the lives of humanity in general—to a much deeper level than is the norm. He needed to become educated in many fields related to spirituality and the sciences.

Accordingly, he felt an urge to attend university, an urge that emanated from his spiritual self because it was part of his life plan. However, what would be most useful to performing his life tasks was a generalist rather than a specialist education. The intent was not to become too focused on any field but to obtain an overview of several fields and to a sufficient depth that he would be able to make conceptual connections between them. So history, art history, literature, philosophy and religious studies all became part of his formal education, to which he added much through his own reading. He also joined a spiritual group to expand his understanding of his psychological make-up and to learn the process of undertaking an extending course in self-enquiry. He then needed to meet his colleague, Peter Calvert, association with whom created the situation for channelling to become a possibility. All these were preparatory steps necessary for him to fulfil his life plan.

If any one of these steps had not been taken, if our scribe had failed to respond to the subtle urges that continuously emanated from his spiritual self, if he had backed out and not acted on them, the drive he felt from a young age would not have blossomed into the spiritually-related activities that now occupy a significant portion of his life. It goes without saying that means we would not be collaborating with our scribe and writing these words you are now reading.

How is responsibility relevant to this? Our scribe needed to be responsible to himself, to his own inner drive. Without the application of responsibility he would not have fulfilled all the required preparatory steps. There has certainly been a trade-off in all this. In order to stay focused on his life tasks certain possibilities normal for human beings were not taken up. Not having children was a major trade-off. Not having the economic stability that is usually pursued in the modern world was another, along with the certainties of occupation that provide people with a grounding for their life. For many years he changed jobs, continued his self-education, and honed his writing skills, but without knowing where his life was headed. He had periods of self-doubt. There were times when others questioned what he was doing, times when he questioned what he was doing and he fell into depression, floundering inwardly.

It is true that many people would have become so uncomfortable in this situation that they would have thrown up their hands and sought something on which to anchor their life. It is also true that our scribe's psychological make-up, bolstered by his store of prior experience, was such that he actually enjoyed this feeling. He enjoyed the feeling of freedom it gave him. The trade-off was a lack of certainty and grounding.

This brings us back to the questions that spurred us into this somewhat long disquisition. Is a person like our scribe special in some way? Is he privileged? Why does he have a spiritual connection that most others don't?

By now it will be clear that the situation the question is probing is not this straightforward. To say that someone is special or privileged is to miss the point that any abilities or talents people exercise, in any field of activity whatsoever, is present because they have chosen to focus on them. They have worked on their abilities and honed them. They have not been gifted their abilities. They were not arbitrarily born with talents others equally arbitrarily were not. Whatever qualities they possess have been developed via efforts they made in past lives. A number of lives. So to the extent that they may be identified as not conforming to the norm, which human social language denotes as special or privileged, they are actually to personal effort. Would that everyone made an effort to become "special" and "privileged" in relation to their own abilities!

In fact, this is what needs to happen for humanity to evolve as a species. The norms of human activity are much lower than they could or should be. Every single person alive can up their game in the context of whatever occupies them in their current life and do it better. By which we mean, more effectively, with more focus, with greater skill, and more responsibly, so the lives of those who are impacted by what you do are enhanced and not degraded. Of course, life is overwhelming, and so much comes at you on a daily basis that it is difficult to sustain a desire to do better. It is often difficult enough just keeping your head above water, especially when you are responsible for others, so doing more becomes impossible. We certainly understand this, having been in the same position often ourselves. It is in this context that inner drives may be understood.

Many people feel a drive to do something specific during their life. This drive leads to them diverge from the norm in the sense that they apply their ability to a greater degree than is strictly required. They attempt to do whatever they do better. As a result of answering the impulses of their inner drive they become what is popularly called special and privileged. Of course, this is in their own way. Yet there are costs and trade-offs in doing so. Focussing on certain aspects of your life means other aspects have to be dropped. This is inevitable, because no one can do everything at once. This is why repeated incarnation is so useful. What you miss out on doing in one life you get to explore in another. An ability you apply in one field in one life you get to develop in another context in a subsequent life. You also get to enhance what you have developed. You enhance your aptitude, you become more adaptable, and you deepen your perceptions so you can see into situations at greater depth. And you become more nuanced in your responses and ways of working. You become better at doing what you have chosen to do. Simply, as is commonly said, you add more strings to your bow.

This is why you make a plan before incarnating: to set up situations that expand on the abilities that are present in your accumulated human identity, to address weaknesses that are also present, and to become better at being a human personality. And, ultimately, as a spiritual identity.

This brings us to another important aspect of the question, an aspect that is unspoken. In asking why others are special or privileged—a question we hope we have satisfactorily answered—another question is implied: Why am *I* not a medium or channel? Why am *I* not special or privileged? Why do *I* not have a powerful spiritual connection? These question could be reworded: Why do *I* not share their drives? Why do *I* not have their responsibilities? Why does *my* life not involve the same costs and trade-offs?

The answer by now should be plain. They have their life, you have yours. They have their life plan, you have yours. They have particular abilities they are working with in this life, you have yours. They have their trade-offs, and you have yours. In another life the situation will be different. They will have other issues to deal with. So will you. If you could stand back and see sequences of lifetimes, as we do, you would appreciate that in fact everything evens out. Statisticians commonly produce graphs that show two lines. One goes up and down tracking the daily highs and lows of something, let's say temperature. One day it's hot, another day hotter, another day the temperature plunges. The result is a jagged progression through the year. A second line tracks the average temperature. It is a much smoother line that rises and falls gradually, representing the average of all daily temperatures as they play out. Your life follows the jagged line as daily, weekly, monthly and yearly events take you up and down, into happiness and unhappiness, success and failure. But the graph for your entire life follows a much smoother track across the years and decades. The same applies to multiple lives. One life you're up, another you're down. But over a sequence of hundreds of lives everyone's average tracking line follows an upward curve. Ultimately, everyone is getting better. In their own way, in their own time, and in the particular situations and fields that resonate with them. This is why you are here. To live, to learn, to develop, to evolve. It is that simple. And that hard.

We are conscious of having answered this question at considerable length. However, it brings up something fundamental to human existence. It also picks out a widely shared anxiety. Everyone wants to feel special in some way. Yet so many people feel the opposite, that they are a failure, that they are unworthy, that they are being left out. The admiration of royalty and celebrity is a manifestation of this anxiety. So is the desire to kneel before religious leaders, to follow a guru, to worship the wealthy, or to eulogise someone who does whatever it is they do, and so are perceived as being special.

We won't repeat here the New Age homily that this isn't true, that everyone is special in their own way. This is an empty gesture for those who feel not only their life is inferior, but that as a human being they are inferior too. Living as an incarnated human being is difficult. Each person experiences their own personal trajectory through the huge number of possibilities available in the human domain. This trajectory is unique. No one follows the same track anyone else does.

Accordingly, we suggest that instead of projecting your anxieties outwardly and comparing yourself to others, it is more useful to focus your attention inwardly, appreciate the abilities and talents with which you are working, note the trade-offs involved, identify the psychological traits that are holding you back, and get on with trying to do what's important to you, and doing it better.

If you can appreciate these aspects of your life, in effect you will lift your head above the churn of daily life and obtain a bigger picture of what is going on in your life. It is not necessary to identify all the details of your life plan, although if you do what we have just suggested major aspects of your life plan will certainly become apparent to you. The fact is, doing anything to obtain a bigger picture of your life than you currently possess is always useful. Putting things, especially painful things, into a broader context often reduces their sting. That is why, for those who wish to seriously dig into what is happening in their life, we suggest you initiate a period of self-enquiry. How to start this process is by looking at what currently occupies your life right now and consider it in the light of what we have just discussed.

It is your life to do with as you wish. You are the one who is responsible for how your life plays out. Whether you realise it or not many options hover before you. Our advice is to look hard at your options and think about what is best for you in your current situation. Then choose what most appeals and follow through. Following through is the big thing. Don't let your anxieties stop you in your tracks. Rather, use the energy provided by your anxieties to take a step forward. Use your anxiety as a motivation. See what you are anxious about as something to use as a springboard to action. Then step over it and walk on.

We are conscious that so much more could be said about this, but we must end here. Our hope is that these few words trigger something in you, our reader, and stir something deep that becomes the beginning of an important next step for you. Because the most important step in your life is always the one you are about to take.

Question 12

Why all the contradictory books, gurus, guidance?

Okay, I get that. But while we're on this topic, what about psychics with their advice on how to live? And the thousands of books about the secrets to success, how to think positively, and all that stuff? There are so many theories and recommendations on how to live these days. Just one example, there are thousands of books on how to meditate, and every one is different! Then there are the gurus, so many of them! Is any of this spiritually derived? If it is, from what source? And how should I navigate through it all? People say I should put my best foot forward, but I feel I need to be careful where I step!

THE GUIDES RESPOND:

The short answer to this question is that for incarnating people to have a diverse range of experiences, a diverse range of possibilities need to be available to them.

In the first book in this series we compared life to a fun fair in which many attractions offer different forms of entertainment and experience. Some people like the competitive attractions, where they seek to win prizes. Others like going on rides that offer an adrenaline rush. Others like having the bejeezus scared out of them. Others like to wonder at acrobatic skills. These are all on offer at a fun fair. But not everyone is attracted to the same thing. Diversity is made available because those who operate fun fairs know not everyone who visits enjoys the same experience.

This principle applies to human existence. People need different kinds of situations and challenges in order to develop aspects of their deep self. When people incarnate they naturally gravitate towards people and life situations that resonate with them. This gravitational pull is pragmatic: it pulls them towards those issues incorporated into their life plan that they need to address. So they may naturally feel they need to perform the role of guru or psychic. Or become an entrepreneur who makes money through the activities of gurus and psychics. Alternatively, they may become someone who happily earns money to pay for interactions with a guru or psychic that they need to grow. So from an experiential perspective, the huge diversity of what is available in life physically, emotionally, psychologically, intellectually and spiritually exists because of the huge diversity of human requirements. Diversity provides all kinds of experiences, which in turn provide opportunities for all kinds of growth.

This is the short answer to the question. But the questioner also asked if that diversity is spiritually derived, and if so what source gives rise to the diversity. To answer this we need to step back and look at human diversity from a wider, spiritual perspective.

Human existence is not unguided. By this we mean that long-term plans are in place, plans that extend not just across years and decades but centuries and millennia. One example of multi-millenial planning is what has been termed the Axial Age. This era began when a number of spiritual teachers, writers, thinkers and practitioners adopted a view of the spiritual domain that was more abstract than had previously been the case and injected that abstract concept into the wider culture in which they lived. Thus Indian meditators introduced the concept of Brahman as an abstract force that powers all existence. In China the related concept of Dao was introduced, in Greece the notion of the One, in Iran the idea of Ahura Mazda. These abstract notions were designed as an alternative to the concept of personal and supernatural gods that were widely worshipped in those times. As intended, the abstract notions penetrated the cultures into which they were launched, offering new concepts on which individuals could build a deepening spiritual understanding.

This widespread activity was initiated at the spiritual level. How it happened was that prior to incarnating a number of people were trained so they could present this new abstract concept into the regions where it was planned they would live. This occurred over many years and involved numerous people. Some individuals were primed to participate in the dispersal of the new concepts through joining spiritual groups, through personal spiritual practice such as meditating, or by writing, preaching, debating, teaching, and so on. If you look at the history of Buddhism, you can see just how many people, living in many different regions and speaking many different languages, were involved in the initiative. That same intensity of activity can be seen in the histories of Taoism, Greek philosophy, Jainism, Sufism, Kabbalah, and so on. All these initiatives were guided. All were planned. All have their own momentums and goals.

The diverse application of a single initiative, such as generating the Axial Age notion of an abstract basis for spirituality, provided extensive, multi-life opportunities for numerous individuals to experience, explore and grow. In this sense the initiative aimed to have a practical outcome, insofar as, like the fun fair, it generated a diverse range of experiential possibilities for incarnating individuals.

But what about the other aspect, that Axial Age abstract notions offered a new understanding for how the spiritual realm relates to the human? Where did the idea to offer this level of understanding come from? It might be thought it was imposed on humanity from above by spiritual overseers. This was not the case. It was actually initiated in response to human beings who, between lives, reviewed what they had just experienced and decided that new cultural conditions needed to be put in place in order for them to best develop their spiritual understanding during their upcoming lives. Because what we have just said may be misunderstood, we will repeat it in another way.

As a result of their multi-life work, a significant number of individuals were uncovering subtle aspects of the relationship between the spiritual and physical realms. Their problem was that the cultures in which they had lived lacked the concepts and words they needed to express their developing understanding. Without appropriate concepts and words no idea can be adequately expressed. So for those evolving individuals to continue exploring the subtle relationships they were uncovering during incarnation, new concepts were required. This is why during the Axial Age many new concepts and words were invented, such as Dao, Brahman, buddha nature, nirvana, atman, and the One, along with a refreshed notion of reincarnation. Their introduction occurred simultaneously across a number of cultures and languages. They proved successful, enabling individuals to share levels of understanding that were subtler than had previously been the norm.

So the initial momentum to introduce subtler concepts did not come from non-human beings. It came from incarnating human beings who felt that as their understanding of the relationship between the spiritual and the physical deepened, the existing cultural frameworks into which they were being born, then largely religious in nature, were proving inadequate. They needed a subtler human cultural environment to express their new levels of understanding. So it was momentum generated by incarnating human beings that established the first stage of what is identified today as the Axial Age.

The next stage was that non-embodied identities listened to what the incarnating individuals were saying, that is, during their between life reviews, and set about generating a plan to create the required changes in cultural conditions. We need to reiterate this point: the plan was made in response to what incarnating human identities decided they needed in order to grow. It was not a change that was arbitrarily ordered from on high, to use human terminology. An initiative was generated in response to changes among the incarnating populace. When human beings face changes in their physical and social environments they make new plans and set them into motion. That is how things also function for those on the spiritual plane.

Who was involved in setting the plan into motion? To be specific, who was involved in generating all the specific situations necessary to initiate a cultural shift as extensive as what occurred during the Axial Age? Three levels of spiritual identities were involved.

One was on the level at which we operate. It involved identities who had completed their cycles of incarnation on Earth and whose prime focus had shifted to facilitating the growth of identities who were still using the process of incarnating in human bodies to evolve. Just as we are now involved in offering new concepts related to human physical and spiritual existence, so non-embodied identities were then involved in creating a new initiative. It could be said they were acting as responsible adults, assisting those working towards their own maturity by helping create environments useful for their continued development.

The second level of involvement was on the human level. Incarnating identities needed to be involved because many things needed to be put in place in order to foster such a cultural change. For example, individuals needed to create life plans that incorporated a commitment to the new notions. Numbers of individuals needed to incarnate together to form groups of practitioners. This occurred repeatedly, over sequences of lives. Some individuals needed to create life plans that incorporated travel in order to disperse the new concepts. And, of course, individuals needed multiple lives to grapple with the implications of these subtle concepts in the context of their own accumulating human identity. So human beings needed to be, and very much were, involved in the multi-year, multi-life and multi-cultural initiative that today is identified as the Axial Age.

The third level of involvement in the initiative is somewhat abstract. This level is beyond the level at which we exist. Identities continue to evolve after they have completed their incarnational cycle on this planet. This will certainly be the case after you have completed your own incarnational cycle. You will reunite with all those who constitute your immediate spiritual family and together you will continue to experience, learn and evolve. For a period you will function as we are now, by interacting with and aiding those who are developing via the process of embodiment. You will then, as we will before you, progress to higher levels of being, of insight, of comprehension. You will also interact with more experienced identities. These identities do not disappear forever into the spiritual beyond. Like us, and like you, they function within spheres of responsibility. Accordingly, they provide their own insights and understanding, thus offering a wider framework again within which an initiative like the Axial Age initially functioned—and, we note, continues to function, more than twenty-five hundred years later. This level of non-embodied identity very rarely interacts directly with those existing on the human level. Rather, they pass on their insights to those at our level, and we pass it on to human identities as part of instituting the overall plan.

This, then, is a somewhat truncated explanation for why there is such a diversity of beliefs, religions, perspectives, teachers, practices, and cultural frameworks. Diverse situations exist because incarnating individuals require diversity to grow. This also explains why pre-Axial Age abstractions remain so prevalent and why there is such a confusion of often conflicting notions—people still need them to work through their previous life experiences and resolve the difficulties that have arisen in relation to them. They also need opportunities to develop an appreciation of the subtler aspects of human existence. No one understands those subtleties immediately or easily. Subtle understanding has to be developed step by step. The diversity of religious and spiritual situations range from crude to subtle precisely in order to provide opportunities and experiences that are appropriate for individual needs.

How do you navigate your way through all these diverse beliefs and practices, with different gurus and teachers contradicting what each other say? You navigate by following your own path. All the contradictory advice results from people being at different stages in their development, dealing with different issues, needing different things, and having different kinds of understanding and misunderstanding.

There are always individuals who are less mature than you and others who are more mature than you. Some have experienced and know more than you, others not so much. Yet those who have lived fewer lives than you may have experienced deeply what you are just beginning to explore. So while their overall understanding is less expansive than yours, nonetheless they may have specialist knowledge from which you could learn.

Accordingly, we suggest you focus on what resonates with you. Use your own inner urges to guide you towards situations you inwardly feel will benefit you and away from those you feel won't. The one caveat we would add to this advice is that you will very likely become aware of urges emanating from your gloopy self. Feelings that you lack what others have, feelings of being left out, of being diminished, are not the inner feelings we are advising you to follow. You need to develop discernment so you can be alert to inner urges or external advice that is not conducive to your self-betterment.

We conclude by affirming, yes, take care as you navigate through life. But don't be so careful that you avoid new experiences altogether. It is through maintaining a balance between the known and the unknown, the safe and the uncertain, the well-worn and the fresh, that you will continue to make progress. Challenge yourself, ask questions, probe. And don't stop. That's how you will develop and grow.

Question 13

Why is my life so difficult?

You make everything sound straightforward. But my life isn't. It contains so much pain and anguish. What did I do, or not do, to deserve this? And as I get older life just seems to get more and more difficult. Am I so thick I just can't get it? I've heard it said we're never challenged with more than we can cope with. That just makes me feel even more of a failure. Does it mean I'm stacking up credits for the next life? Or after this life is over will I just be told to go back and try again?

THE GUIDES RESPOND:

Life as a human being is often difficult. There is no need to underline this point. We agree this is how life can be. The question is, what can be done about it? To this extent, we will treat what is being asked here as a matter of practical psychology.

No one incarnates with the aim of experiencing deep pain. Certainly, many life plans involve addressing emotionally complex situations, usually involving karmic scenarios and righting wrongs one person has done another, and doing so often results in one or more of those involved going through periods of intense anguish and pain. On the other hand, frustration can also trigger other intense emotions, bringing them to the fore of awareness. This difference between pain and anguish being embedded in a situation, and feelings of anguish or pain, buried deep inside, being triggered by an apparently unrelated situation, needs to be investigated and clarified. To understand what is going on inside you you need to get to the causes of your feelings. This is where we return to the topic of self-enquiry.

It is only by observing yourself, watching what happens when you experience intense emotions, seeing what triggers your feelings, then analysing what causes you to respond in the ways you do, that you will be able to understand what is happening inside you psychologically. In order to successfully do this, that is, in order to observe your emotions and follow them back to their causes, several pre-conditions are required.

First, you need to learn to step back internally. This is initially easier to do in a state of at least relative inner tranquility. Such a calm gives you the inner space you need to review the situation that brought up the intense troubling emotions. Pain and anguish are certainly two such emotions, but there are many others, including fear, anger, violence, greed, self-pity, and so on. We suggest you start a journal and record everything you remember about what happens each day. That way you not only create what could potentially become an extensive record of how you act in various life situations, in the activity of writing in a journal you are learning to step back and observe yourself.

There is an art to doing what we are calling *stepping back internally*. The goal is to look at yourself and your feelings and actions dispassionately, as you would observe another person. Of course, from time to time others look at you and comment on what they see. But the advantage you have over everyone else is that you have access to the emotions surging through you. You have a unique position that others do not and cannot have. The ultimate goal is to be able to observe yourself in the midst of actually feeling intense emotions. But this takes time. The first step is to recollect what happened after undergoing an intense experience, then recording it all.

Second, in doing this you need to set aside justifications, denials and judgements. Normally, when people are caught out doing something hurtful to others, and are questioned about it, they react with automatic self-protective behaviour. The four main defensive behaviours are to deny, deflect, justify or attack. When people review their own actions these same defensive behaviours may also come into play. So you might justify why you reacted so intensely, or deny that it's a serious issue, or deflect by claiming it is out of character, or blame someone else or the circumstances. All these kinds of responses need to be set aside when you are recording your behaviours. The aim is to observe and record without being defensive, and especially without judging yourself. Self-judging manifests in you condemning yourself, or saying you are not good enough, or that you'll never get things right. This is not conducive to progress. So an essential part of the self-observation process is quelling all such feelings and thoughts.

All intense emotional responses are grounded in events that happened in the past. So the third step is investigating causes by asking what has triggered your pain, anguish, anger, violence or self-pity. Causes have two principal possibilities: events that happened in this life, often during childhood, and events that happened in previous lives. Frequently key childhood events, especially those that are traumatic, have been planned to enable the individual concerned to work through the consequences of what happened in a past life. However, this is not always the case, with traumatic events sometimes occurring that are outside the life plan.

There are a number of ways to discover causes. One is through memory. That is, you can cast your mind back to childhood and work through what happened. When difficult or traumatic events happen during childhood people create behaviours to cope. Mostly, coping behaviours involve burying what happened, so it may take some effort to remember what occurred. It is possible to use meditation to do so. Dreamwork is also recommended, asking your deep self for a dream to tell you what happened. Joining a self-enquiry group could be helpful, as could seeking the aid of a therapist. All these approaches can help uncover buried memories. It is necessary to spend some time on this process, as there are often layers of responses, each buried under the other. In the case of causes that have roots in past life events, multiple interlinked emotions are involved, which you can expect to take some time to unpick.

The whole point of engaging in this work is to break the cycle of an event occurring, you reacting, and then you feeling the debilitating effect of intense emotions. This brings us to the fourth point, breaking the cycle. This is when you initiate new behaviours that break the old behavioural patterns. Doing so successfully involves stepping in while an established psychological pattern is actually underway and changing the course of what happens. To do this you need to have reached sufficient facility in the art of stepping back internally.

Understandably, this process will appear complex and difficult. It is. But it offers you a way to escape the intense emotions of pain and anguish you are experiencing. You may also wonder if there is a faster fix. There is. You could try saying a prayer, mantra or affirmation to fill your awareness with alternative, more positive, thoughts and emotions. Without energy being fed into negative emotions they will fade. However, the behavioural pattern still remains deep inside you, and it will resurface on other occasions. What we are offering you here, in the process of self-enquiry, is a way to confront and eliminate what bothers you completely and permanently. It involves transforming your psychological make-up. This is very useful work.

Having offered this on what you can do to alter your inner situation, we will now reply to the other parts of the question.

Did you do something to deserve your current anguish and pain? You did. But what you are experiencing is not punishment. It is the result of your own actions and your discomfort with them. You may think we are being somewhat hard-hearted here. However, what you have to remember is that this person you currently are is just one in a long sequence of people. In a previous life you got into a situation that led you to feel psychological discomfort, and you are aware of that discomfort now because your spiritual self wants to deal with it and eliminate its negative impact from your accumulated human identity. So while these intense emotions feel like punishment, that they are present in your awareness is a positive. It is like having a sore leg. The pain makes you aware that something isn't right in your leg. Once you become aware of it you can go to the doctor and get it healed. Without the pain you don't know that something is wrong. The same applies psychologically. Painful emotions are making you aware of a significant issue. The more intense the emotional discomfort, the more urgently you need to address what you are feeling.

The questioner observes that with age has come more emotional discomfort. In fact, as people age they generally go psychologically in two directions. The first is to ignore all negative psychological traits, defending them when challenged. As a result those traits become more deeply buried in the personality. The second is to become more aware of short-fallings. The fact that the questioner is feeling that life is getting more difficult as they age is a tribute to their increasing sensitivity. So no, it is not that the questioner is becoming, as it was put, "thick". Rather, the questioner is starting to delve into the subtleties of human existence and coming to appreciate the depths of what isn't working well and so becoming open to the reality that aspects of their psychological make-up may be improved.

People often feel that something is going wrong with them as they become more aware of life's injustices, or unfairness, or pettiness, or plain ugliness. In fact, they are starting to see more deeply. The trick is not to become overwhelmed by these negative behaviours as you begin to perceive them more clearly. This is where learning the art of stepping back is useful. Stepping back takes the immediate emotional sting out of what you perceive. It allows you to see with clear eyes rather than eyes clouded by hopelessness, anxiety or despair. Of course, being able to do so then opens you up to other issues, like dealing with being able to to see what people are doing to limit themselves, but not being able to do anything to help them. Such helplessness leads to another topic, which we won't broach here.

Are you only ever challenged with what you can cope with? Yes, this is usually the case. We have previously discussed information being released to you on a need-to-know basis. As you delve into any issue, what you need to address and resolve will be made available to you. But for this to occur you need to keep exploring, keep investigating, keep enquiring. If you stop doing so, and instead react according to established defensive behavourial patterns, you'll end up wallowing in your emotions and wondering if you can cope.

By living in such an uncomfortable inner state are you stacking credits for a future life? This is an invalid concept. There is no such system in play. After your life is over, will you be told to go back and try again? This is closer to the reality of reincarnation, but is still not right either.

Incarnation is an incremental process. Life by life you respond to situations in ways that are shaped by your psychological make-up. You respond to some situations well and to others poorly. In some situations you learn your lesson either on the spot or in the immediate wash-up, you adjust your responses accordingly, and you move on to the next situation. At other times you don't respond well, make a mess of things, perhaps hurt yourself and others physically or emotionally, or both, and you don't correct your mistakes. These errors are uploaded to your accumulated human identity to work on in future lives. Similarly, the lessons you learn during each life, and the skills you develop as you put the lessons into place and get them to work positively for you, are also uploaded to your accumulated human identity. All these will be available to you to draw on as required in future lives.

So it is not that you are being rewarded or punished for your successes and mistakes. It is rather that you are building an accumulated human identity for yourself life by life. Life by life you have the opportunity to rectify mistakes, and in the process you develop skills and overcome weaknesses in your human presence. People learn through repetition. Incarnation involves much repetition. But repetition also enables you to perfect skills and develop your talents. The eventual goal is to become loving and wise, to be able to cope in any and all situations, and to develop sufficient inner resources to help others as they themselves struggle with the task of being human.

To conclude, we point out to the questioner that during the course of being human there are tough times and there are beautiful times. Enjoy the beautiful times, but use the tough times as opportunities to develop your inner resources. Don't avoid what is making your life tough. Face up to it, delve into what is causing it, and do something about it. Take it on and wrestle it into submission. Once it is squared away it is squared away for good. And you then have more time, energy and inner resources to expend on creating more beautiful situations, now and in the future.

Question 14

How can I stop being reactive?

You say we need to learn to step back, yet I'm so reactive. When little things happen, when another person does something I don't like, or when things just don't go the way I want, I react. Sometimes it's anger, often just frustration. Sometimes I react verbally, other times I keep my reaction inside my head. How can I change this? How can I stop being so reactive?

THE GUIDES RESPOND:

We have observed elsewhere that human existence involves living life up close and personal. Earlier in these pages we noted that attachment and identification are what keep you immersed in the events of your life. As we also remarked, this is necessary because it makes life immediate and real.

Life is not a pretence. It is no illusion. No one is living as people were depicted in the film *The Matrix*, in which human beings were asleep and dreaming all that happened to them. What you are experiencing is not a dream. You really are here living through all you feel, think and do. That is the whole point of human incarnation.

Yet a paradox is involved in this. Because while one part of you is immersed in human existence, enjoying its pleasures and suffering its pains, another part of you stands aloof, observing all that occurs. This part the ancient Indian meditators called the witness. It is the atman, the self, your spiritual identity that remains detached and separate throughout the course of your life. We commented in the previous book in this series that no one sends all of their spiritual identity into a body. Some part, often the larger portion, remains separate from the portion of your spiritual identity that is immersed in your body. So the reality is that you are simultaneously inside and outside your body. Yet, and this is the paradox, you are not aware of this. For you as an incarnated individual, your experience is that you are here, and whatever else you are is not part of what is happening. It is distant, so distant, it feels inaccessible, perhaps even non-existent.

Accordingly, we now recontextualise the question in the light of this being your actual circumstance. It means that one part of your awareness is functioning in lockstep to physical reality, to which attachment and identification tie it emotionally and psychologically. This is the part that reacts when some other person, or a trying circumstance, rubs you the wrong way. Yet in the very same moment another part of you, your spiritual self, stands apart from what is happening. So the question can be rephrased: how do you shift your everyday awareness from being wholly immersed in the trials and tribulations of daily life, and attach it instead to the detached witness, the part of you that participates in human existence without getting reactively caught up in it?

Psychospiritually, this is what is being asked. The answer echoes what we discussed in our previous response, bringing us into the sphere of practical psychology. And that returns us to the practice of standing back internally.

In *Practical Spirituality* we identified one of the major tasks of being human is mastering the art of incarnation. Everyone has to learn how to function effectively as a spiritual identity occupying a body. This is not to imply that people need to learn how to stand back internally so far that they no longer participate in human interactions. That is not what we are saying at all. The practice of learning to stand back—which is a skill you need to learn in order to master the art of incarnation—is wholly internal. It is within that you need to learn to stand back. In fact, its most accomplished practitioners are able to do so while in the midst of very trying situations. This is why we propose it as a solution to being reactive. When people react they become energetically lit up by negative energy. This commonly gives rise to anger and frustration, certainly, but also to resentment, self-pity, violence, sexual desire, fear, and the like. The whole point of learning to stand back within is to be able to do so while the fires are burning and sparks are flying all around you. As would be expected, this is not an easy skill to develop.

In the previous response we discussed keeping a journal in order to document what happens to you and how you respond. Doing so is a stepping stone towards learning to step back, because in the act of writing you are doing so in a cool, detached, recollected state. We noted this is sound training for learning to step back within. The next step is what the questioner has asked: how do you stay cool and detached in the midst of daily heat? This involves another big inner step.

We are assuming that you are not some kind of super person who is able to snap their fingers and instantly shift their awareness into the witness, into their spiritual self. That is not a realistic expectation, neither from our perspective of you, nor, from your perspective, of yourself. Rather, stepping back within is a skill that, like every other skill, has to be learned, one step at a time. It is in this developmental context that we offer our practical advice on learning how not to react.

By keeping a journal you will learn of particular situations in which you react more than is usual for you. What these situations are varies from one person to another. It depends on past experiences, the traits dominant in your psychological make-up, and the situations that repeatedly present in your daily life. We suggest you initially focus on just one situation. This may be at work, at home, while taking part in sport, or when you are out at night playing.

Start by analysing what is going on in this situation. Is it one particular person who rubs you the wrong way? If so, what is it about them that does so? And what is it in you that reacts? If it is a situation, then analyse it, again with an emphasis on what psychological traits in you cause you to react.

What you will learn is that you have some pre-set behaviours that push you to react in ways you naturally act out. You need to examine where these behaviours came from. The vast majority will come from childhood events, when to defend yourself you engaged in certain coping behaviours, such as running away, hiding, crying, striking out, complaining, blaming others, or eating. As you grew older this childhood coping behaviour was socialised in different ways, again depending on your new life circumstances and on other psychological dispositions active within you.

This level of self-enquiry is a necessary first step that enables you to understand what is happening within you. Incidentally, it also takes the heat out of your responses, as engaging in a process of self-enquiry is already helping you step back inside yourself and observe your feelings and behaviour as if they belong to another person. In doing this you are training yourself to step back inside yourself.

Next you need to interrupt the cycle of something happening to you and you reacting with a preset response. This requires you to have presence of mind in the moment that the troublesome stimulus is occurring. From this perspective, it makes no difference whether you react aggressively and physically, whether you lash out emotionally, or whether you withhold your external response and keep your response within. A reaction is a reaction, whether it is external, wholly internal, or, as is usually the case, involves elements of both.

In order to interrupt the cycle of stimulus and reaction pre-planning is a useful strategy. From your journal you will already know that a certain person or situation stimulates a certain reaction from you. Pre-planning succeeds due to the principle that being forewarned is to be forearmed. By this we mean that your journaling enables you to anticipate when the troublesome stimulus will happen again and to be ready for it when it does. What you need is to have something else planned, so when the troublesome stimulus occurs you can move your attention away from it and onto whatever else you have planned. For example, you may say a mantra or a prayer in order to occupy your mind and so reduce the emotional engagement and therefore the reaction. Or you may divert the other person involved onto something else. Or you may simply walk away. Whichever you select, the purpose is to have some other activity prepared, alternative to your usual reactive behaviour, towards which you can direct your attention.

It is likely that at first you will be so attached and identified that you will miss the warning signs that lead into the troublesome stimulus, so you end up getting caught up and reacting. If you do fail, put it down to experience and try again, on the next occasion. It's like learning to drive a car. At first you have trouble remembering all you need to do. But with practice you master each skill, then you one day discover you can do the several things you need to all at once. Similarly, with breaking the cycle of reaction. Repeated effort leads to success. You will recognise the telltale signs that the troublesome stimulus is on its way, you will remain alert to it in the moment, you will engage in your preplanned alternative activity, and as a result you will succeed in shortcircuiting the reaction. Having achieved success with this one reactive scenario, you can then move on to whatever else concerns you. Step by step, you will be able to recognise, grapple with, and change all your reactive psychological pre-sets.

To widen this discussion somewhat, we observe that behind the practice of standing back within is another skill, popularly known as mindfulness. This is a skill that is initially developed during meditating. Mindfulness in its current form has its roots in the Buddhist Eightfold Path, which links concentration, effort and mindfulness into three aspects of the one practice. That is, to be mindful your mind has to be focused, which in turn requires directed effort. To successfully practice mindfulness you need to make a concerted effort to focus your mind and hold that focus. Several practices can help you develop this skill. Prayer and saying a mantra, in which words are repeated over and over, is certainly useful. This keeps all other thoughts at bay and enables you to develop one-pointedness.

When you become able to control your thoughts, the next step is to learn to sustain inner silence. This involves stopping the flow of associative thinking that automatically flows through the untrained mind. The practice of inner silence is relevant to stopping being re-active. When you react one of the things that happens inside you is that particular thoughts become active and dominate your mind, just as certain emotions become active and dominate your feelings. One-pointedly sustaining a mantra or prayer interrupts the automatic, re-active flow of thoughts. Learning how to stop your thoughts altogeth-er, and turn off the flow, is even more effective. Without thoughts, no reactive thinking is possible.

Psychologically, mindfulness is an externally directed quality. That is, you gather your attention within, and you then direct it in a sustained, conscious way towards whatever situation you are current-ly in, or towards the people with whom you are currently interacting. In this sense, holding a sustained state of mindfulness will certainly short-circuit your tendency to react.

In the past this was largely the way people worked against their reactive psychological pre-sets. It was certainly effective, given that when people faced a troublesome stimulus they learned to shift their attention to another level within, including into the witness. How-ever, there remains a flaw with this procedure. It is that any reactive psychological pre-set existing in the psyche has not been addressed. That means that if the individual becomes inattentive, which will hap-pen from time to time, they will slip back into reacting automatically, according to their psychological pre-sets. In ancient times this created problems in monasteries, ashrams and zendos. The problem was, seekers were not addressing and eliminating the psychological weaknesses at the core of their accumulated human identity. This is why we are proposing this psychological approach.

Self-enquiry doesn't rule out traditional practices such as prayer, meditation and mindfulness. They strengthen your connection to your deep core and extend the resources you have to draw on. Nonetheless, they are just part of the answer.

People often want there to be lists of approved and non-approved practices. Our perspective is that with all these types of endeavours, it is never an either-or situation. You don't have to choose one and not the others. Our advice is rather that you are best off doing what you can. Consider how much time and energy you have at your disposal. And whatever you decide to do, do it consistently. Engaging in practices once in a blue moon, even though done very intensely, rarely leads to greater success than committing to some smaller task, but doing it consistently. In the parable of the tortoise and the hare, the tortoise won out. This is not always the case, because there are many factors affecting the course of a life. But it does provide a useful rule of thumb.

Underlying everything we have just been discussing is one further practice to which we wish to draw your attention. This is the practice of presence. Being present involves engaging your inner witness, your spiritual self, in your daily existence. By implication, this means being present physically, emotionally, intellectually, psychologically and energetically as well as spiritually.

Try being present in each and every moment of your day. It's not at all easy to do. Your everyday awareness naturally becomes attached and identified during the course of whatever is happening. In contrast, being present in the moment requires you to be aware that a part of you is the witness, and that you *are* witnessing, while simultaneously you remain fully engaged in the activity in front of you. This is a skill that sits at the pinnacle of the art of incarnation.

The practice of presence is the ultimate psychospiritual goal. Being spiritually present involves activating the witness, acting lovingly and wisely, while drawing on all the resources you have developed within your accumulated human identity.

We appreciate that this is beyond the vast majority of people. But this is the big picture. In order to reach that pinnacle you need to start somewhere, with something practical that you can put into action. This means you need to start with something small that is part of your daily existence, something you can recognise, understand, and do something about. Dealing with one reactive behaviour is such a starting point.

Yet every small thing has its place in the wider picture. So while your spiritual practice may begin with just one small thing, something that may not even appear to be spiritual at all, it actually leads you into something bigger, that is all-encompassing.

We state this to give you encouragement. If you address one small reactive behaviour, and eliminate it, you are actually developing psychospiritual "muscles" that will stand you in good stead, enabling you to accomplish other much greater things. Clearly, doing so will be to your deeper, ongoing benefit.

Accordingly, we commend the questioners' desire to learn how to stop being reactive. As the saying goes, a journey of ten thousand miles starts with just one small step.

Question 15

Can I eat my way to enlightenment?

Why are you emphasising the psychological so much? I always thought diet was really important. I also understand that spiritually it's better to be vegetarian than eat meat because of the vibrations we ingest with the food. And anyway, not having massive livestock farms is better for the environment. What do you say? Will being vegetarian help me get more in tune spiritually? How significant is diet to becoming enlightened?

THE GUIDES RESPOND:

This is another interesting question that highlights a number of issues it is necessary to understand in order to fully appreciate humanity's place on this planet. It also highlights the level of confusion that exists, given people want to do what is best for themselves and the biosphere but don't have sufficient facts at hand to make an informed decision. This confusion results from false assumptions. We'll start our answer by addressing two key false assumptions.

First, the question is formulated in terms of either/or. Is it better spiritually to be vegetarian? Or is it better to eat meat? This dichotomy is too simple, in fact, too simplistic, to capture the complexity of the situation that exists on your planet. The question also offers a false dichotomy, suggesting we are emphasising psychological make-up over diet. Besides the fact that we have done no such thing, because we haven't so far discussed diet in any of the comments we have made via our scribe, the questioner's underlying assumption is that life involves making simple choices. This is an error.

Humanity is addicted to binary thinking. Binary thinking includes common dichotomies such as her and him, us and them, good and bad, right and left, East and West, conservative and liberal. This type of thinking is too simplistic to capture the complexities of human existence. We have been urging our scribe for some time to write on this topic, as binary thinking is a form of conceptualisation that is to everyone's disadvantage. This can be seen to be the case when binary concepts are linked to winners and losers, and everyone tacitly concedes that winning eliminates the need to consider what the winners have done that is wrong, by which we mean the harm they did to others on their way to succeeding. You see this in many spheres of human activity, where people too readily grant others the right to do what they want merely because they are winners.

To make an observation humourously, people's self-pacifying psychological traits—which includes subservience, lazily avoiding thinking deeply, and worshipping dominant personalities—leads them to "eat up" what they told. And here we specifically link psychology and diet, because, of course, what sustains you is never simply a matter of food. The questioner is correct to observe that vibrations are ingested with food. And if vibrations are ingested, then that makes them food. So rather than psychology and diet being separate and juxtaposed, they actually overlap.

To reiterate, nothing in your life is simply a matter of this-that, either-or, because what are supposed to be opposed binaries are always interlinked. Neither exists without the other. We won't hammer this point any further, but leave you, our reader, to look at the world around you and consider this for yourself.

The limitations in binary thinking is made clear when we consider the second false assumption behind the question. This has to do with the relationship between the spiritual and physical. Humanity, and we are referring now to contemporary humanity, assumes there is a difference between the spiritual and the physical. We disagree, on the grounds that we know, based on our direct observations, that this is not the case. Furthermore, what we perceive responds to a further assumption, that it is more spiritual to be vegetarian than to eat meat.

How we see things is that everything on this planet has a spiritual identity associated with it. Earlier we introduced the concept of elementals, spiritual identities who associate with physical places. We also commented on other types of spiritual identities who associate with insect and animal species, and yet others who associate with crustaceans, fish and dolphins and whales. More spiritual identities associate with every species of fauna. In other words, every place, every species, and every individual biological creature and entity, has a spiritual identity of some kind associated with it. These spiritual identities differ in function and in energetic bandwidth, and also possess their own distinct and unique energetic signatures. So whether you eat an animal or a plant, or whether you prefer to eat one over the other, strictly speaking, from a spiritual perspective, you are devouring a living entity which has a spiritual being associated with it. So by eating anything you are taking away the opportunity for that spiritual identity to associate with a physical creature. Of course, the spiritual being knows that the creature or plant species it is associating with will die, so you are not doing anything that harms the spiritual being. Our point is that this complexifies the question of whether it is better spiritually to eat plants or animals. Here's another related issue.

One way of viewing life on this planet is in terms of food chains. Every plant, insect, fish and animal lives in a particular environmental niche. Its body is adapted to living in this niche, into which it is born, feeds, grows, has progeny, and dies. This environment necessarily has to provide nutrition. So each plant and creature feeds on other plants or creatures in that niche. And, in turn, when it sheds parts of itself, and when it eventually dies, it provides nutrition to those others in the niche. To offer an example of one food chain, a plant sucks nutrition from the soil, an insect feeds on the plant's leaves and another extracts nectar and flies off carrying pollen, an animal eats the insect, another animal eats the first animal, and the remainder of the eaten carcass breaks down and returns nutrients to the soil. Everything living is born into a niche where a food chain operates, and it necessarily plays its role in that food chain. This is how life on this planet proceeds. It cannot not be so.

As a species, humanity sees itself as being at the top of all food chains. But, of course, this is only because human beings have wiped out most of the major predators they once had to fend off. We refer particularly to big cats and bears that fed on human beings up until relatively recent times. Of course, sharks still occasionally feed on a surfer or swimmer. So it is not that human beings are at the top of all food chains, it is just that human numbers have exploded and so have overwhelmed the environmental niches other species occupy, which has sharply reduced the numbers of those species, especially those that once preyed on human beings. Human population growth has reduced so many species' environmental niches that species have been wiped out. As is widely known, today many more species are under threat.

So, to turn the question around, we would say that instead of asking if it is more spiritual to eat plants rather than animals, we suggest it is more pertinent to ask: Should human beings respectfully allow all species and their associated spiritual identities space to live? And as would be expected, based on what we have just stated, our answer is yes, absolutely. From a wide-view perspective, it is unspiritual to continue a course which is devouring environmental niches across the planet and, as a result, eradicating entire species.

This is an important point. We titled this book *How Did I End Up Here?* with the intention that you, our reader, would situate yourself in the middle of that "I". On the one hand we are addressing the notion of life plans and the principal elements that shape anyone's life. But we also wish to address the wider issue of how humanity has ended up in its current situation. This particular question usefully opens up a wider conversation about how humanity has ended up here and now, at this point in history, in which its population is exploding and almost no one is facing up to the implications of the situation. As we write this through our scribe, climate change is exercising many people's minds. Despite public discussions on this topic dating back several decades, the extent of the social and economic changes that will have to be made to reduce greenhouse gases has hardly sunk in. Many people, in fact most of the world's population, still don't wish to engage in the thinking required. Yet greenhouse gases are just a symptom of a much larger, underlying problem. That problem is overpopulation.

The point we have just made, regarding species' environmental niches being overwhelmed, is a symptom of overpopulation. The recently publicised problem of plastic being present in every part of the biosphere is similarly a symptom of overpopulation. The seas being over-fished, forests being cut down, soil quality deteriorating, waterways being polluted—all have their root causes in overpopulation. Humanity has many problems, but this is the biggest elephant in the room that very few are looking at. With the world population having been two billion in 1900, and expected to reach eleven billion by 2050, this is the key issue that shades everything else.

It is highly unlikely that sufficient momentum will build over the next decade or two to address overpopulation. In that case climate change will likely lead to currently inhabited regions becoming uninhabitable. Famine and conflict over diminishing resources could potentially kill millions. It is also possible that in the resulting politically stressed situations nuclear strikes will be initiated. Regions on the planet, mostly urban regions currently densely inhabited by human beings, would then be rendered uninhabitable for the foreseeable future. And, of course, millions more would die. It is even possible that instability would grow to such an extent that it initiates a nuclear winter, during which clouds cover the skies, hiding the sun and reducing the temperature. If this happened the majority of the planet's living creatures could die off. There is a precedent for this in the Earth's history, with volcanic explosions several times initiating mass extinctions.

We are not saying that major conflict or nuclear winter will happen. We are just making the point that these scenarios are possible. But it can definitely be stated that if population growth and rising global temperatures continue on their current tracks, the Earth and all species on it will be radically effected. How radically will not be known until it happens.

Our point is that this stark possibility provides an opportunity for human beings to take responsibility for their role in what is happening and come together to address it. This situation may be viewed as humanity's biggest collective spiritual challenge. It is spiritual because the physical and spiritual are interlinked.

In earlier responses we commented on your life being the result of choices you previously made. If you are in an awkward, unhappy, satisfying, relaxed or terrible situation, it is one you yourself have selected in order to evolve as a spiritual identity. The same applies on a planetwide scale. Humanity as a species has made certain choices in the past that has led to the current situation. And just as individuals often have to feel intense psychological pain before they become motivated to do something about their unhappy life, so humanity as a whole is starting to experience environmental pain.

The question is, how long everyone will allow it go on? How bad will things have to get before humanity acts? That is the test. It's a test in the sense that responding to it denotes a significant step in humanity's evolution as a species. The test is spiritual because it involves everyone, at the deepest level of their awareness, facing up to the reality of their life situation and the life situations of those who are to be born in the ensuing years. And we include *all* the planet's species among those who are yet to be born.

Will people open their eyes? Will they engage their minds? Will they acknowledge the hurt they are generating for other people and other species? Will they acknowledge what they are creating for their own descendents? Will they take responsibility? Will they do what is right on a planetwide scale? These are not just ethical questions, they are spiritual questions. They get to the heart of you being a conscious being living in a period of significant change. What are *you* going to do? How are *you* going to respond?

We appreciate we are being somewhat confrontational here. But these are serious issues and someone needs to start acting. And if not you, then who?

Having stated this, we return to the question and address it in less general terms. The question asks if it is spiritually preferable to be vegetarian rather than eat meat. In terms of environmental resources, it would clearly be better for the planet if land was no longer being taken for farming animals and was left in forest. But stopping forest being cut down at their current rates requires more than just individuals not eating the livestock raised on the newly claimed land. It involves taking a stand against deforestation. And it involves a call to reduce population growth to reduce the need for more food and so pasture. So while a decision not to eat meat is a first step, the next step requires activist involvement.

This is one part of the question. The other part has to do with personal spiritual growth. Behind the question is the assumption that in order to develop spiritually you should not kill creatures for your food. We have commented on this in relation to food chains. It is not intrinsically more spiritual to step out of a particular food chain. This is because all creatures, plants as well as animals, have sentient existence, and all are associated with a spiritual identity. So it makes no difference from this perspective whether you eat plants or animals. Living beings are being devoured and their associated spiritual identities connection to the physical through that individual being is cut off. This is the wider metaphysical context. However, there is still the question of whether ingesting plants is better for a person vibrationally than eating animals. Once again, there is no straightforward yes-no answer.

In humanity's evolutionary past eating the protein present in meat not only helped individuals survive in difficult conditions, giving them more energy for less effort, but the protein also aided the growth of their brain. So meat protein has had an essential role in the species' survival and development. But, of course, there are many more sources of protein today than there were for humanity's ancient forebears. So as long as access to sufficient proteins can be sustained, is there a continued need to eat as much meat as people have in the past, or even to consume meat at all? Related to this question is the argument, raised by Buddhists and others, that animals killed in a state of fear may convey negative emotions to whoever eats their flesh. There is also the misery of the animals themselves as they are brought into slaughter houses where they can smell blood and so realise what is about to happen to them. Surely, the question implies, eating food killed in such negative circumstances must be anti-spiritual? These are all excellent points that have much value to them. To answer this multi-layered question we will head off in a direction that might not immediately appear to be appropriate, but trust us, it will help us provide a pertinent answer.

Impressions tether you to reality. We previously discussed bandwidths, noting that different spiritual species live within different energetic bandwidths. Impressions exist within a certain bandwidth. For example, the sensation of the sun's warmth on your arm, or the impression of red light on your eyes, each exist at particular electromagnetic bandwidths. The human perceptual apparatus operates across a range of bandwidths. Perceptual bandwidths vary between species. A dog can hear frequencies a human cannot. On the other hand a human being sees colours that a dog does not. So while most of the human and canine perceptual bandwidths overlap, enabling them to share impressions, there remain differences in sensory ranges, which means each species receives sense impressions that the other does not. This much is clear. But there's a larger aspect to this. There's the issue of what each species does with the sense impressions it receives.

Each species has a central nervous system that processes and responds to sensory input. The biggest organ in the nervous system is the brain. Human beings have a large brain with includes a primitive, reptilian level that is responsible for basic feeding, survival and reproductive responses. All species possess this function in simpler or more complex forms. Mammals have the evolutionary addition of a mammalian brain, and many species also have a neocortex. In the human species the neocortex is large and layered, adding high level functioning that facilitates complex emotional, psychological and intellectual responses to sense impressions. Basically, human beings can extract more information from sense impressions than can other species because they have a more complex brain. This is straightforward.

However, there are other kinds of impressions. There are impressions that exist on bandwidths that are not physical and so not able to be received via the senses. We noted that dogs can hear frequencies of sound that human beings cannot; they are out of the human sensory perceptual range. The other kinds of impressions we are referring to are similarly outside the human sensory perceptual range. Yet they can be perceived. This is because human beings have more than one perceptual apparatus. The second is energetic. It functions on the bandwidth of the energetic self. As we noted earlier, the energetic self exists in parallel with the physical body, being superimposed over it. Just as the physical body receives impressions via its senses, so the energetic self receives impressions via its energy nodes. Energetic perceptions are not part of standard education programmes so people tend to have less facility processing energetic impressions. Nonetheless, energetic impressions exist. And they have an influence on everyone's awareness.

When you interact with your pet, clearly you are interacting on a sensory level. But let's say you are playing with your dog or riding your horse. In addition to your physical connection you also feel an emotional connection. What is actually happening is that you are sharing impressions on the energetic level, via your energetic self. Your pet also has an energetic self, so it is receiving your emotional "vibes" via its energetic layer. Hence your awareness is receiving two bandwidths of impressions, one via your body's physical senses, the other via your energetic nodes. These impressions are on distinct bandwidths. Energy stirred in the energetic self can and does seep into the body, and visa versa, as we will presently discuss. But the impressions themselves exist on their distinctive bandwidths. So to return now to the question, what does this have to do with being vegetarian?

When you eat food your two perceptual systems are operating. So you physically taste and chew the food, then you swallow it and your digestive system extracts nutrients from it, eventually expelling what remains. What is extracted from the food remains in your body. Mostly this involves nutrition, but if something poisonous was in the food it is also ingested and poison enters your system, impairing your body's functioning until the poison either dissolves, or is counteracted, or is expelled. The same process applies energetically.

Your energetic system interacts with whatever energetic component is attached to the food you eat. Usually, the energetic component is negligible. But if an animal suffered emotionally before it died, the energy generated can cling to the flesh and still be present when you eat it. We must add some caveats to this statement. Rather than the moment of death, what is more likely to generate a negative energetic component to animal products is their treatment throughout their life. So free range, free farmed animals will have a far more wholesome energetic component than factory farmed animals that live their lives in cages, cramped and uncomfortable. It is also the case that how food is cooked, and the energy of those handling the food as it is prepared, may have a greater impact on foods' energetic component, as it sits on your plate, than what happened when the food was harvested or killed. There is the old saying that food tastes better when the chef prepares it with love. Energetically, this is so.

To answer the question, yes, there is an energetic component to everything you eat. But it is not as straightforward as the questioner assumes. Food's energetic component has several sources and layers, the weighting of which change according to circumstances. So there is no one answer that applies to all situations. We encourage everyone to adopt wideview perspectives and set aside one dimensional analyses and attitudes. Everything is connected. And the connections are multi-layered. The world you live in overlaps physically, energetically and spiritually. The overlaps play into each other in complex ways, in fascinating ways—or, at least, we find it so. We hope you will too.

We conclude these comments on food with the observation that manifesting a positive intent over food before you eat it helps dissipate any negative energy attached to it. Saying a prayer or grace is traditional. However, these will have no impact unless a positive intent accompanies the words. So while expressing gratitude for your food is beneficial, we suggest not just thanking your God, nature or the Earth, but actually directing your gratitude towards the species you are eating. This will be beneficial for all. The important part of acknowledgement is always your intent. So you don't actually have to pray. You can silently gather your gratitude within, in whichever place you prefer, and direct it towards those we just pointed out. This action will have the desired beneficial impact.

How does this work? We have previously discussed cultural streams. Each species on this planet has its own cultural stream. These streams exist each on their own energetic bandwidths. When you intend gratitude towards any species it becomes an energetic message that is added to that species' cultural stream. This is relevant due to the action of symbiosis.

When microbes, plants, insects and animals co-exist in an environmental niche, feeding off each other, using one another for shelter and reproduction, their deceased bodies returning minerals to the earth to feed future generations, those involved are existing in a symbiotic relationship. They are physical intertwined. As we have pointed out, they are also energetically intertwined. And not just through the energy they extract physically from each other, but through their overlapping energetic layers. Then there is a third level of symbiosis. This involves all the spiritual identities associated with the species in that niche. These spiritual identities exchange mutual goodwill via the energetic layers of those with whom they associate. But, beyond this, there is also the energetic contribution made by each individual plant or creature to its species' cultural stream. When human beings add their goodwill to that stream, in the form of gratitude, it contributes to and helps sustain all these multi-levelled symbiotic relationship. All involved benefit from that.

Accordingly, we recommend that whatever you eat, whether plant, insect, animal, fungus, fish, crustacean or mineral, you send your gratitude to the environmental niche, to the individual animal, to the species, and to the spiritual identities who are overseeing their existence. That intent is your best spiritual contribution to the continuation of a healthy, multi-layered biosphere.

Finally, there is the question of whether diet contributes to your spiritual development. From what we have just said, it will be clear that spiritually your intent when eating is more significant than the food itself. You make eating a spiritual activity through your intent. The actual food is of secondary importance. Whether or not to be vegetarian we leave for you to decide. There are certainly many arguments in favour of it, including environmental and general health reasons. We note that people's diet today includes many processed foods, the excessive consumption of which can only be considered unhealthy. Again, we leave it for you to decide what is best for you personally. As far as the planet-wide perspective is concerned, you as an individual need to be healthy in order to contribute to your species' continued healthy existence.

Question 16

What about rising allergies and autism in children?

I appreciate your comments on eating. But what about food allergies? And autism and learning disorders? They are on the rise as a proportion of population. Is there a reason for this? I am curious whether it's related to the growing population. The population was four billion in 1974. In 2018 it's headed towards double that. Are people reincarnating so quickly, and the conditions of modern life changing so rapidly, that they're reacting negatively to it? Related to this, I have read about indigo children, who are supposed to have behavioural issues due to their gifts. They're called indigo because that's the colour of their aura. Related to them are star children, with gifted crystal and rainbow children added to indigo. What's with that? Then there's the idea that extra-terrestrials are volunteering to incarnate on this planet to help us transition into a more positive culture. The problem is many haven't incarnated on this planet before, so suffer psychologically from being here. It all sounds too much. Or is there something to it?

THE GUIDES RESPOND:

To answer these questions involves a great deal of information. A book could be written in response. However, our scribe doesn't have that much time and the intention here is to answer in just a few pages. So we will range over the issues involved while leaving much unsaid. We apologise in advance for these restrictions.

We begin with the wider incarnational context into which these questions need to be situated. Every spiritual identity associating with physical species on this planet comes from elsewhere. Not one originates from here. Why? It is because they are spiritual and this planet is physical. Spiritual beings come into existence in what, in human terms, may be called another dimension. We prefer to call it another bandwidth, because all reality is one, it just exists as a continuous, overlapping series of bandwidths.

Accordingly, all spiritual identities on this planet, including you, our reader, come from elsewhere. You are, as is said in human terms, a migrant. This is not your place of origin. This planet is a place to which you have travelled for the purpose of experiencing, learning, growing and evolving. This exact same purpose is behind all the other spiritual identities present on this planet. They are here to experience, learn, grow and evolve, each in their own particular ways.

This is not the only physical place to which you may migrate. Every spiritual identity now incarnated in a human body has seen other worlds, enjoyed other physical states. This is one option between lives: to explore other places. Some even decide to physically associate with creatures living there. As a result you may have associated with creatures on other planets. It's not certain that's the case for each reader, but it is a significant possibility.

Why would you travel to another world, whether for the equivalent of sightseeing, or to associate with creatures non-human in nature? For some it is curiosity, to see something different. After all, incarnating life after life into the human world is demanding. This is a wonderful yet fraught place. It is full of much beauty, but human interactions are difficult. There is much negativity, much that is demanding, sometimes too demanding. Understandably, individuals occasionally need a little time out. Going somewhere else to have different, less intense experiences can be refreshing, cleansing. So that is one reason individuals choose to visit other worlds.

Another is to test particular faculties, for example, telepathy, or artistic ability, or empathy. Cultures in other worlds have different cognitive configurations to the human, and different balances of cognitive functions. So going elsewhere can provide an opportunity to develop an ability in a social environmental that is less demanding and more supportive than is offered in the human world. This is a second reason you may have travelled elsewhere, to undergo what, in effect, is a short-term workshop to enhance your skills.

These kinds of travel are not random. It could be said that just as there are migratory routes across this planet, in which people travel to one place then another before arriving at their final destination, so there are migratory routes in the spiritual domains. To put it simply, experienced identities who share your basic spiritual nature have explored alternative physical places and so are in a position to make recommendations to you based on what they know of those places and what they know of you. Their knowledge and expertise enables them to function as guides, helping less experienced individuals understand what is beneficial to them and pointing out the virtues of the available possibilities. In another book we have likened these guides to travel agents. Their expertise may be relied on to offer useful advice. Of course, where an individual chooses to go after being advised remains entirely up to them.

What this means is that if you wish to have a change of scene or pace from incarnating on this planet, and you are offered a choice for going somewhere else, whatever is recommended is on an established migratory route. Others similar to you have been there before. They know what the deal is regarding being there, whether you are sightseeing or spending extended personal time.

For an extended period of visitation to be possible, a crucial prerequisite is that the cognitive and cultural configurations of the physical creatures on that planet resonate with you. This is because you as an individual incarnating in the human world have accumulated particular experiences and skills. So there has to be a sound fit between your expertise and the new world you are visiting. If you travel somewhere where totally different knowledge and skills are utilised to those you have accumulated here on Earth, you'll find yourself struggling to make a connection between your awareness and the new body with which you are now associating and the physical and social environment it inhabits. So unless you wish to make a serious, multi-life commitment to learning how to exist in a world totally different from the human—a commitment some do actually make, but so rarely as to be negligible in terms of what we are discussing here—the world you select is required to resonate substantially with your human cognitive capacities and the associated skill sets you have developed.

When such a world is found, which is compatible with human experience, multiple individuals end up travelling there, eventually in sufficient numbers for that place to be identified as being on the human migratory route. Furthermore, just as on this planet you need to travel to one place in order to reach other, so migratory routes frequently involve a number of worlds, with preparation in one world being required before an individual can move on to another which is a little more complex. This is one reason why personal development is crucial.

Only when you reach a certain level of expertise do you become able to take advantage of what is available in other worlds. This applies to physical as well as non-physical worlds. In order to travel on this planet you need a ticket; without a ticket you don't get through the door. Similarly, to travel to other worlds you need a ticket, which is your accumulated developmental state. On Earth you work at a job to earn money to buy a ticket. On the level we are referring to here, you work on your identity to earn entry.

Let's bring this back to your life here and now. Before you were born you did some extramural learning. The purpose was to strengthen skills in preparation for your upcoming incarnation. Actually, it will have been a range of interlinked skills, because no skill stands alone. Let's say you intended to focus on being a musician. You have, in your accumulated human identity, developed a musical skill set in previous lives. But, as we noted earlier, other negative traits will have also come to the fore during those lives. These could involve self-doubt, feelings of rejection, being arrogant in success, and so on. So between lives you will have looked at a bundle of related skills and traits and prepared to address them collectively in your upcoming life. But, of course, people rarely have just one skill set to develop. This preparation may be repeated across two, three, ten different skill sets, all of which you prepare yourself to work on during your upcoming life.

It is in this context that going to another world could be of use. It would enable you to look at and work with the skills and related psychological issues you intend to grapple with from another perspective. It may even be that two or three lives in another world could be useful for jolting you out of a difficulty you are having, helping you work through a combination of traits that you aren't managing to resolve in the human world. Usually, between incarnations, people go to school to learn about what is involved and to get advice, and this is sufficient. But sometimes what is needed is another type of learning experience. So time in another world becomes useful. Essentially, it becomes an opportunity to address issues with which you are stuck.

What we are attempting to do by discussing human beings' travel to other worlds in this way is to normalise the process. That is, we are attempting to show that you, as a spiritual identity, have one home base, this planet, where you incarnate regularly, it being the main physical world you use to experience, learn, grow and evolve. However, you also occasionally travel to other worlds. Some you visit for time out, to relax, and some you visit to engage in inner work. The first treats other worlds as holiday places, the second as places you travel to to attend workshops and learn something new. Doing both is normal on this planet. They are equally normal on the spiritual level.

Naturally, we are aware that this may be read as science fiction. We can't deny this. But why do you think science fiction is so popular? We know that many understand, deep down, that what we are saying is true. Note, however, that in all we have said we haven't mentioned flying saucers. When, between lives, you go to sight-see in another world, you do so entirely spiritually, without a body, so you have no need for a physical vehicle. Similarly, when you attend a workshop in another world, it may involve associating with a body, but there are actually several ways of doing so. You may incarnate as an individual in a body. Alternatively, you may piggy-back on another being, who gives you access to their awareness as they experience life on that planet via their own body. Or you may be there energetically, with impressions arriving via an energetic body rather than through physical senses. You may do the equivalent of auditing, being present but observing without taking part directly in what is happening. And there is always the possibility of imbibing from that species' cultural stream and learning what you need to by drawing on their collective experiences.

This, then, is what is done by you and spiritual identities like you, who associate with the species homo sapiens sapiens, inhabiting human bodies on this planet, which is their home base world. But what about other spiritual identities, for whom this planet is not their home base? Just as human identities go to other worlds to sightsee, or to do workshops, or to have a different experience of physical life, do other identities come here to do the same?

As would be expected, the answer is yes, most certainly. Just as other worlds are on migratory routes for human identities, so this planet is on other species' migratory routes. But, to reiterate, no one turns up anywhere by chance. Just as you have a reason for going to other planets, so these identities have a reason for being here. As you would also expect, and just like yours, their reasons are various.

So, with this background information in place, we are now in a position to address the questions. We begin with a consideration of autism, learning disabilities and food allergies among children that over recent decades educationalists and psychologists have recorded as growing as a percentage of the population. People with expertise are noticing a change in the population. Why, then, is it occurring? It has to do with the nature of individuals' accumulated human identity.

Each time you incarnate you have a choice as to which positive and negative traits existing in your accumulated human identity you will draw on and engage in your upcoming life. The full range of choices is complex, as are the reasons you choose the ones you do. We have discussed this at length in our *Channelled Spirituality Series* so won't detail the process here.

What we will say is that one of the chief criteria for choosing to address a certain group of traits is opportunity. That is, you need a suitable social environment to explore certain traits. You can't develop horticultural skills if you are born into a desert and will have no way of escaping to lands where gardens are cultivated. You need a suitable environment to explore specific skills and traits. This is the case with those children who are presenting various learning disorders, food phobias and autism. There currently exists a supportive cultural environment where careers as educationalists and psychologists have become possible. Such careers were not possible in previous centuries and cultures. The upshot is that a culture of psychological diagnosis and treatment has developed in which people are gaining the expertise to recognise phobias and disorders and are learning how to treat them.

As a result there is currently a supportive social environment in which individuals can address the self-limiting psychological traits that have become embedded in their accumulated human identities, traits that got there as a result of how they responded to experiences they had in previous lives. So the rise in the incidence of individuals presenting with phobias and disorders is due to pragmatic opportunism. Individuals who have embedded psychological issues they need to address now have a conducive social environment in which they can be helped to address them. As a result, they are taking advantage of the opportunity.

There are several issues of relevance to this situation. One is that you, our reader, have many positive and limiting traits in your accumulated human identity. After incarnating multiple times, you will have accumulated from all these lives so many skills and traits that you cannot draw on them all in any single life. So, again pragmatically, in each life, or to be more accurate, during a series of lives, you focus on particular packages of inter-related skills and traits. Which package you choose depends on various factors, including what is available in whichever social environment you are planning to incarnate into next. So what is important to you now, the issues you are dealing with, and the possibilities you are exploring, have been chosen by you according to what is available wherever you were born. Similarly, if you have travelled to other parts of the planet, beyond your birth place, it is because of the possibilities such relocation has opened up. In the vast majority of lives this is all planned before incarnation.

So those who are presenting phobias and learning disorders today will have held back addressing those issues until a suitable family and social environment became available. In the distant past, when people lived in villages, it was the shaman or medicine man or woman who had the role of diagnosing and treating psychological ailments. Of course, they lacked current psychological knowledge. However, they did have, and shamans today continue to have, their own kinds of expertise. Part of that expertise involves being able to draw on knowledge of human psychology that they developed in previous lives.

Today the world's population has increased and people have migrated from villages to cities. In this environment there is no official role for shamans, their roles having been replaced by psychologists, teachers, doctors, and so on. Individuals who have an innate bent towards nurturing and curing people, who in the past took on the roles of shaman and medicine man or woman, are currently incarnating as educationalists, social workers, psychologists and so on. This is the flip side of those who have incarnated in order to work through their phobias and disorders: those who have developed skills as curers have simultaneously incarnated to assist them. It is a pragmatic solution, with each side having the opportunity to experience and learn what they need in order to keep developing.

Why do so many people possess phobias and disorders that require treatment? To answer that question we need to go back many thousands of years. When human beings lived in small villages or nomadic tribal groups, disagreements sometimes occurred between individuals. Occasionally a domineering person attempted to take over the group, or actually did so, to the distress of others. But in general those living in small groups worked out their disputes without much trauma. This social situation began to change during the Bronze Age. People in areas with growing populations came together to live in towns. Some towns grew into cities. Large populations developed the specialist roles of bakers, potters, weavers, farmers, soldiers, and so forth. Cities also needed rules, and people to enforce the rules. As a result classes of people formed: workers, soldiers, priests, an aristocratic elite, and kings. Kings inevitably wanted more territory, and the materials available in other territories, so armies were formed, battles fought, and the beaten peoples were enslaved. Large numbers of people were coerced. Many were imprisoned, tortured, executed. As a result, huge swathes of populations were negatively impacted. Ongoing wars continue to have a similar impact on millions today.

Every individual alive today has been tormented, and very possibly has tormented others, during their past incarnations. For millennia violence has been woven into the fabric of human interactions. Individuals have watched their families die, have died themselves from violence or famine, been locked up, tortured, raped, and treated harshly and with casual indifference by those in a position to inflict physical and psychological harm. As a result, everyone has had negative experiences. Reacting to these experiences has resulted in intensely felt, debilitating, psychological traits: suspicion; deep-seated fears; tendencies to strike out, turn away or withdraw; profound discomfort with sexuality; and the whole raft of phobias and disorders that people develop. Everyone works through their past issues in ways that suit them. Currently, given parts of the modern world offer opportunities to identify and address phobias and disorders, many individuals are taking advantage of the situation to work through what troubles them.

We have two further points to make in relation to this. The first is that if you have a child or close family member who is working though autism, food phobias or learning disorders, try to see the big picture. It is a useful opportunity for you to help another by expressing your love and support. But it is also an opportunity to develop understanding, to look behind your loved one's external behaviours and come to appreciate their deeper causes. There is no need to share what you know with the conflicted person. What we are suggesting is entirely for your own education. If you are able to use the process of self-enquiry we advocated earlier, but turn it onto your loved one, and you are able to learn what is driving their behaviour, you will not only be personally edified, you will be in a more informed position to help them. In later years, and depending on circumstances, you may even be able to share at least some of what you have learned. Naturally, that is a matter of personal judgement. And, as we said, that is not the primary purpose of engaging in deep enquiry. It is for your own education regarding the nature of being human.

The second point is with regard to your own strong negative reactions. Take note of times when you powerfully react against anything that happens to you. It may be in response to what someone says either to you or to someone else. It may be another's gesture, a set behaviour, something they always do. It may be something you do, your own repeated emotional reaction to the same situation. It may manifest in feelings you suppress, behaviour you act out, words that unthinkingly come out of your mouth. Keep a note, because doing so offers you an entrance into understanding one of your own phobias or psychological disorders.

Phobias generally have their origins in particular incidents. For example, if you have a phobia regarding spiders, and no incident stands out from your childhood that could have caused that reaction, if you just react instinctively against their presence, it is very possible that you had extensive negative experiences with them in a prior life. For example, you may have been locked up in a prison cell full of spiders for years, often felt them on you, even woken with spider webs draped across you. It is understandable that after such an experience an individual would become phobic towards spiders. Other phobias are more layered. For example, many individuals are instinctively offended by sexist behaviour. Again, if that response doesn't originate in earlier life experiences, past life experiences are likely to be the cause. In the case of being averse to manifestations of sexism, it may be that the individual was the victim of sexism in a previous life to such a degree that the resentment, suspicion or anger that rose in them in reaction shaped that life's personality and subsequently was uploaded to the individual's accumulated human identity. They are manifesting the emotional reaction again this time round so it may be worked on. Alternatively, the individual may have been highly sexist in a prior life and so is now seeking to counter that imbalance, which makes them sensitive to others' sexist behaviour and attitudes.

Disorders tend to be more complex. Where phobias generally hinge on a single issue, disorders involve compensatory behaviours that work on two or more levels and so require some unpacking. For example, learning disorders may involve issues with authority. The individual may have been coerced in a previous life, either by an overbearing individual or through an excessive regimentation of their life, and now they are unwilling to submit themselves either to others or to an ordered environment. Autistic children who seek to create order are trying to live within their own order so they don't need to live according to someone else's. On the other hand, an individual with autism could be deflecting their own attention from a deep-seated issue they are having difficulty addressing, but they need to deal with the deflecting psychological attitudes before they can address the core issue. There are many possibilities.

As a result, disorders are difficult to get to the bottom of and so address. Many well-meaning people attempt to do so today using chemical inputs to modify behaviour. This should always be a last resort. It is like having a boil. Suppressing the symptoms doesn't make the boil go away. Sometimes the boil has to be lanced and things have to get messy before progress is made. Learning how to delve into past life issues will definitely aid those who are attempting to understand and treat deep-seated disorders.

Everyone has disorders of some kind. It is just that most people manage to remain functional. But sometimes people go off the rails and do something horrible that shocks those who thought they knew them. They behave in this manner because some powerful emotional attitude burst up from their depths and they weren't able to contain it. Usually this is because they had been attempting to suppress what lay behind their feelings rather than acknowledge and address it. Bubbling magma can only be suppressed for so long before it overflows.

This is why whenever you feel a powerful negative reaction we suggest you make note of it and, when the time is right, delve into it. Some kind of psychological issue will lie at the bottom of it. It probably won't be powerful enough to drive you off the deep end, but if it is present in your personality it is there for a reason: because your spiritual self wants to use this life to address it. We recommend you do so.

In advising this we are not suggesting you walk around with your disorder on your sleeve. It is a personal and not a public matter. Talk to yourself via your journal. Or join a group that facilitates personal reflection. Certainly utilise a process of self-enquiry. Identify what is churning away inside you, how it manifests, what lies at the heart of it, and replace it with positive feelings, thoughts and behaviour.

What about those children who are called indigo, crystal and rainbow? How do they fit into this? Some experts level criticism at parents who maintain that their child falls into one of these categories. They say the parents are claiming their child is so gifted that she or he is having difficulty coping with everyday life. The experts assert the parents are not owning up to their children's problems, trying to explain away their negative behaviours by emphasising their child's positive abilities. We are averse to making general statements of this kind. Each family situation needs to be addressed on its own terms. Of course, some parents only want to see the best in their children and to avoid what is worst. On the other hand, some professionals are programmatic in their responses and rely too much on generalised diagnoses, which prevents them from seeing what is really going on.

It is claimed that indigo children are so named because psychics saw their auras and perceived them as unique in colour. Is this really so? As is said, we don't have access to those case files. And it is not our role to go looking for them. What we can say is that everyone has an aura, which is part of their energetic self. All auras contain various colours, and those colours change according to circumstances. Illness impacts on auras. So do extended negative emotional states and heightened states of awareness. While many people want those they love to be special, claiming they are unique due to the colour of their aura is ultimately not a useful distinction.

Finally, what about non-human spiritual identities volunteering to be incarnated on this planet to help humanity develop, but struggling to do so, having their own issues with phobias and disorders? We are aware that this theory extends to there being three waves of volunteers, with the first wave having incarnated in the 1950s. Is any of this true?

We have largely answered this earlier. Just as you, our reader, will have visited other planets, either to relax or to take part in what is, in effect, a workshop, so spiritual identities whose home base is elsewhere come here to spend shorter or longer periods of time. However, the same criteria we mentioned with respect to your visits elsewhere applies to their visits here.

This planet offers opportunities for experience and learning. Spiritual identities who are domiciled in other worlds may use these opportunities to further their own growth. Many opportunities exist because life here is varied and complex. Spiritual identities come here to experience the opportunities on offer. However, not just any identity can do so. The pre-requisite is compatibility of experience, cognitive abilities and skill sets. To be clear, we will repeat what we said earlier.

When you incarnate for a time anywhere, or associate with a physical species in whatever way, there needs to be a basic compatibility of experience. If, in experiential terms, you are a six year old and they are a fifty year old, then you are not going to learn much of value from them. They are too advanced for you. What is required is a compatible experiential base. The same applies to other spiritual beings incarnating here. They need to be at a similar experiential level, not just to blend in but in order to take part in what is on offer. If they are a master musician and everyone on this planet is still learning to play *Chopsticks*, they won't learn much. So what they need is exactly what you need: a situation that is basically challenging, but that involves tasks that are neither too easily carried out nor are too difficult to complete. So basic compatibility of experience is essential.

What also needs to be taken into account is compatibility of cognitive capacities. For those whose home base is elsewhere, and so have consistently inhabited the bodies of a non-human species, their psychospiritual development has largely occurred within the bounds offered by that species' cognitive faculties. So when they travel elsewhere to inhabit a different species' body, such as a human body on this planet, the new body's cognitive faculties need to match those they have long inhabited. If this isn't the case they won't be able to function in that body with any degree of facility.

Third, compatibility of skill sets is required. Skill sets are an extension of cognitive faculties. So a similarity of cognitive faculties means the skills on this planet will naturally match those they have previously developed. However, the human world offers cultural and social contexts that differ from their own. So while skill sets are similar, the social contexts in which they are applied are different. This provides the challenge and the reason they come here.

That non-human spiritual identities are here occupying human bodies means several things. First they are not really non-human. The two sets of identities have much more in common than not. They are sufficiently similar to be what is termed kissing cousins. Second, that they have found their way here means that non-embodied explorers have scouted out the possibilities and made the match. As a result, this planet is on the migratory route of these non-human individuals. Which means, thirdly, they haven't started coming here just recently. They have been doing so for millennia, just as individuals who identify as human have been been visiting other worlds for millennia.

However strange all this sounds—and we are aware it will sound exceedingly strange to those for whom these ideas are new—that is what is happening. Furthermore, visiting planets that are not a spiritual identity's home base is an entirely normal activity for those who wish to test themselves, develop their current skill levels, and evolve.

Finally, is there some master plan that involves the spiritual identities coming here from other places? In particular, are they are here to aid the advancement of the human species? We will answer these questions on two levels, the collective and the personal.

We noted earlier that human beings have a tendency to exaggerate. Sometimes the exaggeration involves overstating what is happening, to make a situation bigger or more dire than it is. At other times the tendency is to understate, to diminish the significance of what is happening. The impact of overpopulation, and the current collective tendency to ignore it and its implications, offers an example of understatement. An example of overstatement is offered by humanity's apocalyptic stories. Some religions, and we make note of Indian religions in particular, have adopted a cyclic approach to human history. This view considers that history repeats in periodic cycles. Other religions, including Zoroastrianism, Judaism, Christianity and Islam, postulate an end of days scenario, in which a God-stoked apocalypse is supposed to eventually engulf the world. God will then appear to revive decomposed bodies, reward believers, punish unbelievers, and set all things right. This is fantasy. We commented earlier about the over-simplification of binary thinking. This is simplistic binary thinking notched up to the nth degree.

Today many people have shifted this type of religious expectation into a secular, technology-driven context. Those who add extra-terrestrials into their world view are waiting for what is termed disclosure. This is supposed to be a game-changing period when governments will disclose the presence of extra-terrestrials among you and present to all the agreements that past governments have made with them. This scenario, involving a revelatory expose, matches religious believers' apocalyptic exaggerations.

Here we pause to respond to a thought that has just entered our scribe's mind. It is the slogan from a popular sci-fi television series, "I believe." That is an entirely appropriate thought in the context of what we have just discussed. Beliefs provide the basis of much speculation and exaggeration regarding what is going on. Unfortunately for those who take refuge in "I believe", belief is of negligible use when you are attempting to delve into the nature of reality, whether on the level of your life or on the level of this planet as a whole. Rather than "I believe", we suggest a more appropriate slogan is, "I enquire." Belief is passive whereas enquiry is active. If you want revelatory insights, there is no point passively waiting for them to arrive. Knowledge never just arrives. You have to go digging for it.

On a number of occasions we have observed that knowledge exists on a need-to-know basis. There is no point getting knowledge you can't do anything with. Especially when there is other knowledge, that would actually be of direct use to you. To offer an example, a Paleolithic hunter-gatherer would have no use for plans on how to make a mobile phone. First he would need to learn about radio waves, electricity, complex metal smelting processes, batteries, signal repeater stations, and much else. He would also need a use for the mobile phone. Without a use there is no point having it. Similarly, you have no use for knowledge about things outside the sphere of your experience. And if you were given such knowledge, you would have no appreciation of the wider context into which that knowledge fits. Before humanity is ready to learn bigger picture stuff it collectively needs to carry out the necessary preparation. That preparation begins at the individual level.

Your own spiritual self reveals deep knowledge to you when you seek it. But you need to be strong enough to handle what you uncover, because revelatory knowledge, whether about yourself or others, can be difficult to handle. Often it takes people years to prepare themselves inwardly before they are ready to receive deep insights into their own past. So knowledge is uncovered on a need-to-know basis by those who are ready to receive it.

Does this mean we are saying there is no plan involving the presence of non-human identities on this planet? No, we are not. As we said earlier, non-human identities are here because it is useful to each one personally as they experience, learn, grow and evolve. That is certainly what could be termed a plan, an all-encompassing developmental plan that involves multiple worlds, guides, individual travellers and human counterparts who aid them in their efforts. Yet rather than there being just one plan involving all the identities currently associating with this planet, there are numerous plans.

We gave the example earlier of planning with respect to what is called the Axial Age. Much planning on many levels, from the big picture to intricate details involving what happens to individuals during their lives, has been involved in that initiative. The planning began several thousand years ago and remains under way at present. We also previously drew attention to the expansion of the human brain. This required a genetic modification. As a plan it also extended over many Earth millennia and involved numerous individuals. These books are part of a plan to share information, which again involves many thousands of individuals. It began some decades ago and will continue for hundreds, if not thousands, of years hence. Each mystical tradition also has its own plans in place. So do religions. And many mediums are working in accordance with their own plan, their life plan, as well as within another wider plan, or plans, that involve others.

As we said, there are numerous plans in play. And you only find out about them on a need-to-know basis. Not because great secrecy is involved, but because you have your own issues to deal with in this life, and it is much more productive for you to focus on them than to chase down chimeras, especially when they are exaggerations of something someone partly understood, didn't understand at all, or made up to feel better about something they actually had no clue about.

This has become a very long response. And, as we said at the start, much more could be said. But this much was needed in order to respond to the questions in a way that is sufficiently informative to make sense.

One of the difficulties in sharing this kind of information is that so much that people read and repeat is piecemeal. As a result a little information is shared, but too much is left out for the piecemeal information to be satisfactory. In addition, the gaps in piecemeal information that is otherwise basically sound are often filled in with guesses, personal misapprehensions, fearful projections, and wilful embroiderings. As a consequence—and now we are being quite up-front regarding what we are doing in offering these words via our scribe—one of our primary roles is to gather information that is floating around in various circles and normalise it. That is, our role is to show how certain things that are considered weird and out-there have an element of actuality to them. Our aim is to shave off the exaggerations and speculations and explain, in rational and pragmatic terms, how such things occur.

We hope our readers find what we are sharing both illuminating and useful. From our side of the communication link this is certainly proving a fascinating exchange!

Question 17

Did I physically experience energy as fright?

I recently dreamed I was in the kitchen of a house well known to me. At the table sat a close friend. Seated beside her was a woman who was leaning close into her. The woman looked strange, pale and glowing. I had never seen her before. I was also aware I was the only one who could see her. Concerned, I flicked a tea towel at her to warn her to back away from my friend. The tea towel passed right through her. In response, the woman leaned back in the chair, looked right at me, and smiled. At that moment I woke, feeling intensely frightened. The fright actually felt like a shock of energy that was tingling through my body. It went in a wave from my head and down my torso, causing all the hairs on my body to stand up. The wave was like an electric shock and passed up and down my body three or four times. Lying in bed, now wide awake, the tingling fright stayed with me for some time. I had known I was in a dream, nonetheless it felt very real, like I was actually there in the house. After reading what you said about the energy body, it seems possible that what my body experienced as fright was actually energy passing to it from my energetic body. Is that what happened? Did I physically experience energy as fright?

THE GUIDES RESPOND:

Our scribe lives in New Zealand where there is currently discussion among experts in social services and transportation of a need for joined up services. That is, they acknowledge that there are not single solutions to the problems they face, that many factors are involved, and addressing those factors requires different departments and services to work together in a coordinated fashion. Only through joined up activity will the sought solutions be achieved.

The same applies to this question. Joined up understanding is required, bringing together several different aspects of human functioning in order to explain what happened in this dream and its aftermath. We will begin by discussing the nature of dreams.

Dreams are real. That is, what you experience when dreaming is a real experience. It is just real in a different way to what you experience while engaged in everyday life. In order to clarify what we mean we have to return to the concepts of electrophysical and electromagnetic. To recap these concepts, they refer to bandwidths of reality. The human electrophysical experience, by which we mean your experience of yourself as a physical being, partakes of only a narrow portion of what exists within the entire electrophysical bandwidth of reality. For example, sub-atomic particles exist within the electrophysical bandwidth, but you don't experience them. Similarly, certain sounds and smells are physically present but they exist beyond the human range of hearing and smelling. The same applies to the electromagnetic waves. The human perceptual range perceives the visible light spectrum, but this spectrum is itself a narrow band of the total electromagnetic spectrum. Hence it can be said that everyday human experience involves interaction with narrow portions of the electrophysical and electromagnetic bandwidths.

This is one point that has to be appreciated before we can discuss the way that dreams are real. The other involves your personal perceptual range. Individuals interact with and utilise the bandwidths available to them as human beings in different ways. We emphasise *human beings* because what we are discussing is with respect to the human experience of reality. In order to provide you with illuminating material, we need to speak from your point of view, not ours. As a human being you are grounded in everyday reality. This is the physical world you wake into each morning. It is where you eat, drink, laugh, cry, work and play. You engage with this world via your everyday self. This would seem to be a straightforward notion. However, it is not, because your self actually has five layers. These consist of the biological, socialised, essence, energetic and spiritual selves. Your everyday self consciously draws on these five selves to varying degrees. At different times different balances occur within your everyday self, depending on circumstance, your desires as you pursue your selected activities, the desires of others you are interacting with, and the level of reality that you plug yourself into it.

Plugging in is an appropriate metaphor here. You plug yourself into what is happening around you and draw energy from it in the form of impressions. Impressions take many forms: sensory, emotional, intellectual, sexual, energetic, and so on. Your everyday self absorbs these impressions and uses them to operate through the day.

So your everyday self is plugged into everyday reality. But the breadth, narrowness and intensity of your engagement with everyday reality continually alters. You may narrow your attention to focus on a task at hand and so not notice sounds, such as the bus passing in the street or the knock at the door, you would normally notice if you weren't so absorbed. On the other hand, in your focused state you are identifying details and so become aware of subtle interactions that you wouldn't normally notice. In effect, this means that what your everyday self absorbs from the world varies according to the way it is plugged in. The kind of attention it is using, the parts of the layered self that are engaged, the level at which each is engaged, and the balance between them—all this contributes to the narrow bandwidth of everyday attention that you continuously direct towards the world around you. We fear this explanation has become somewhat abstract so will give an example to make what we are saying more concrete.

When you wake in the morning your first task is to plug your awareness into the immediate world around you. Perhaps your bladder is full, so you need to go to the toilet, which is followed by ablutions. This is all physical. But then while you're showering you start thinking of what you have to do at work, or you remember a person you're catching up with, so the socialised self becomes engaged. Or perhaps your day starts with turning on the radio or television and hearing the current news, which you listen to while preparing a drink. Again, these activities involve engaging your socialised and physical selves. Perhaps you are listening to a news item that interests you and one of your children enters the room needing help. The attention of your everyday self, which was involved in drinking coffee and listening to the news, now switches to the child. You put down the coffee, stop listening to the news, and direct your attention to helping your child. Alternatively, you could try splitting your attention and half listen to what your child is saying while also listening to the end of the news item. Then your spouse enters, says something that requires a response, and you are forced to disengage from the news report entirely and pay attention to both your child and spouse.

Another scenario is that immediately you wake up you walk out onto the decking. This is because you are on holiday, in the mountains or on a beach. During the working week you wouldn't pay any attention to the outside environment. But here you are in a different environment and your senses are switched on, noticing colours, smelling the air, feeling the sun or wind on your skin. Your everyday self is engaged in another perceptual mode, very different from its normal mode of functioning. A typical week day begins with breakfasting, getting the family and yourself ready, then leaving your residence and engaging with the day according to a rigid time frame. But on holiday those time frames don't apply, your attention doesn't need to fixate on the usual routines, so your awareness becomes open to impressions it ordinarily has no time for.

This is how everyday awareness shifts focus and expands and contracts. One of the reasons human beings have survived so well on this planet is because their awareness can so easily expand and contract, and so rapidly shift from one field of activity to another. It is an ability that makes human beings extremely adaptable.

The flip side of this is that modern life requires awareness to slot into narrow lines of perception and interaction. Repeatedly trundling along the same lines of interaction, which by adulthood is what people do, has the result of dulling your layered self, keeping it focused on just a narrow range of its total possibilities.

Becoming spiritual begins with breaking free of this constriction on your awareness, shifting into new modes of perception, which is achieved by opening up new facets of your layered self. Basically, it could be said that becoming spiritual involves plugging into new aspects of reality and so obtaining new impressions, which in turn gives you information regarding new possibilities, new tasks and new perceptions.

Where do dreams fit into all this? Dreams are a non-everyday perceptual mode in which everyone participates. Whether you wake up remembering your dreams or not, you dream each night. Clearly, dreams are not real in the same way that a table or a wall is real. They can be touched by your hand, whereas you cannot physically grasp a dream. But this doesn't make dreams unreal. It just means dreams exist on a different perceptual modality. They engage your attention on a different bandwidth to the table and wall.

Part of the problem in dealing with a topic like dreams is that people have very constricted views regarding what constitutes reality, which in turn narrows their idea of what is real and what is not real. Dreams are real, they just involve a perceptual mode different to those you use everyday. As we noted, in your everyday life you regularly switch perceptual modes, from listening to the radio to empathising with your child to becoming impatient with your spouse to getting frustrated with the toaster for not working properly. These events involve your biological, socialised and essence level selves, and so are real to you on electrophysical and electromagnetic bandwidths. In contrast, dreaming engages your energetic self. This is the part of you that dreams. Or to be more accurate, your energetic self is where your awareness is situated within your five-layered self when you dream.

As we observed regarding your everyday existence, the attention of your awareness easily shifts between different people, situations and events. But what isn't readily appreciated is that in doing so your attention is also shifting between different perceptual modes. To reiterate this point we'll reuse the earlier example. You could be listening to the radio and processing it inside your head. Your processing could draw on memories of news you previously heard on the same topic, so intellectually you connect the items. Or you may react emotionally to the news item because you don't like what has been reported, or because a certain politician, who you either favour or dislike, is involved. So listening to the news involves one of these two possible perceptual modes. Then your child enters the room upset because she has spilled toothpaste on her top. You immediately go into empathetic mode, soothing her distress, then into practical mode as you solve the problem. This switching happens constantly. Throughout the day everyone is switching perceptual modes without thinking about it. Everything your awareness interacts with is equally real, whether it involves voices, memories, ideas, toothpaste, your loved ones, conversation. The point is you relate to each using different perceptual modes.

Dreaming is the same. It involves different perceptual modes to those you use in everyday existence. But that doesn't make dreams unreal. They just occur in a bandwidth of reality that differs from the electrophysical bandwidth your everyday self normally plugs into.

Having stated this, a logical question forms: What are you actually perceiving when you dream? In everyday life you interact physically with people and objects. Even intensely felt emotional and internalised intellectual interactions have their basis in physical reality. So what aspect of reality do you interact with in dreams? There are actually a number.

Reality contains numerous bandwidths. When you dream you plug into a small number of those bandwidths. Each bandwidth requires a different perceptual mode. So just as you switch between perceptual modes during everyday interactions, so you switch between perceptual modes when you dream. You experience and think of dreams as all being the same, because they are "just a dream", but in fact all dreams are not the same, and neither are the perceptual modes you need to plug into them. We'll explain.

One common type of dreaming is what we will call diffusing overloads. During the course of the day various tensions build up within you. These could be emotional, such as becoming frustrated with another person, or physical, such as a build-up of pain, or sexual, and so on. When you sleep one of the processes that occurs without you noticing is that your body self-repairs. With the body and its brain being unplugged from the external world for the time, energy normally directed externally becomes available for the body to use to smooth out, as best it can, the tensions that have built up in its internal processing. This is an automatic process that is built into the body's biology, working automatically in the same way that the digestive and the auto-immune systems work automatically.

Self-repairing functions much like a valve that opens up when there is a build-up of steam, allowing the unneeded excess to escape. If it didn't escape the engine would start to overheat, and could eventually explode. So part of the body's self-repair process involves letting out excess energy that has built up in the form of tensions. To some extent this letting out occurs via dreams. We say to some extent because tensions can also result in chemical build-ups, build-ups in muscle tension, and build-ups in the edifice that is false personality. These tensions cannot be relieved via a dream. But tensions we will identify here as psychic tensions can certainly be let out via dreams. So this is what occurs.

How is psychic tension let out? The tension manifests as a dream that plays out, then dissolves. Just as steam let out via a valve dissipates into the atmosphere, so the energy that is creating the tension dissipates into the local biosphere, where it dissipates. Low intensity emotional and sexual tensions are dissipated this way, whether you remember the dream or not. As we said, it is an automatic process.

However, when you wake remembering such a dream—which happens to most people reasonably frequently, especially when they are replaying and letting out the previous day's frustrations and inter-personal niggles—you are using a perceptual mode that is close to the everyday. Close, but not exactly the same. To explain we'll draw an analogy with watching television.

A television show involves performers doing what they do physi-cally and emotionally and being recorded. The recording transfers their physical activities into electromagnetic data. After processing the data, which involves editing, sound-mixing and so on, the show is broadcast in the form of an electronic signal. As a viewer you then watch an electromagnetic version of what was originally physically performed. Is what you are viewing real? Yes. Is it real in the same way as the physical activities? No. One is physically real, the other is electronically real. Each involves different perceptual modes. Yet your response to what you view is real. They are each just real in different ways.

This is similar to what happens when you have a dream that re-sults from tension overload. The tension that has built up within you during the day gets processed by your cognitive system into data in an electromagnetic form. The data then sits inside your psyche as a region of tension. While you are sleeping, as part of its self-healing process, the body automatically seeks to open a valve and blow out the excess energy. This occurs via a dream. Hence, your dream can be thought of as a processed electromagnetic version of what physically happened to you during your day.

Where a television show and your dream differ is that during broadcast the television show's electromagnetic signal is retranslated into pictures and sounds your senses perceive. In contrast, the electromagnetic signal that constitutes your dream remains in electromagnetic form. The signal plays out and the tension the signal embodies is released into the biosphere, where it dissipates. That is, unless you wake remembering the dream. If you keep hold of the tension, allowing it to continue churning inside you, then it hasn't been released. It is then reabsorbed and remains inside you as psychic tension.

The perceptual mode that is involved in this process sits very close to your normal everyday perceptual modes. It is the closest to the everyday range of any of your dreaming perceptual modes. We don't intend here to explore every perceptual mode that is engaged during dreaming, but we will move in a progression from everyday modalities.

The next level of dreaming involves communications from your spiritual self. This could be seen as the inverse process to what happens when your body seeks to diffuse the build-up of psychic tension. Your spiritual self itself at times becomes frustrated with you as you bumble your way through tasks, or when you choose to avoid tasks it put into your life plan before you were born. This leads to a build-up of spiritual-level tension—this is a somewhat crude characterisation of what occurs, but it will do for our purpose here. Your spiritual self responds to its frustration by sending you reminders, at the level of your everyday self, of what you should be doing. Or, conversely, it reminds you of what you should stop doing. These reminders may appear to you in dreams. Such dreams are only effective if you wake up remembering them. So that is built into the process: first your spiritual self injects a reminder in the form of a dream, then it prompts you to wake at a crucial time so you'll remember the dream. In this way the information passes from your energetic self, which is involved in the dreaming, to your everyday self, which needs to act on the information.

Between lives everyone learns how to pass on information from their non-embodied spiritual self to their embodied everyday self. In fact, it is a skill you need to acquire early in your incarnational cycle, so you, at the level of your spiritual self, are able to communicate with you at the human level. Communication is needed via dreams because not everyone is able to meditate, and neither does everyone live in cultures where learning to sit quietly and listen within is taught as a way to communicate spiritually. On the other hand, everyone dreams. So dreaming provides a communication channel that potentially works always and in all situations.

This, by the way, is another reason we suggest you keep a journal. Many dreams have to do with releasing tension, letting off steam. As such they may not be significant. But if particular tensions keep repeating in your dreams, it suggests there are unresolved issues in your life and in your reactions that need to be looked at. In that case having written records of dream materials is useful. If your spiritual self is sending you reminders of what you should do or should stop doing in relation to those tensions, then recording dream communications is imperative.

One of the issues with dreams is that no matter how vivid they are in your mind when you first wake up, they tend to fade away. Over the course of your lifetime you remember very few of your dreams. This is because of the different perceptual modes that are involved. As we said, dreams occur in the electromagnetic bandwidth. They are perceived at the level of your energetic self. In contrast, you live your everyday life largely within the electrophysical bandwidth. During the day you can switch your awareness into the electromagnetic bandwidth, but it involves unplugging yourself from physical activities. This is because, as neurologists have observed—an observation with which we concur—the human cognitive system can only handle a limited number of inputs at any one time. We discussed this earlier with the example of trying to listen to the news while your child is upset and your spouse is asking a question. You can't field all three inputs and give them equal attention simultaneously.

Immediately after you wake from a dream, your energetic self is active and your essence self begins processing the information in the dream, wondering what it means. At this moment the biological and socialised levels of your self are quiet. What is happening is that you are functioning in an energetic modality that is quite different to your everyday modalities. If straight after you wake, and still being in that energetic modality, you write down what you remember of the dream, you will be able to include in your account the subtleties that are apparent in that perceptual mode. But if you don't write it down, perhaps telling yourself that you'll remember it and record it later, what happens is that as you get ready for your day your perceptual mode shifts into your normal everyday modes. In these modes your biological and socialised selves dominate and your energetic self falls into the background. Because you are using a different configuration of your layered self, the subtle energetic level you perceived earlier is no longer accessible to you. As a consequence the memory of what you perceived in your dream fades and becomes inaccessible. You need to be in an energetic perceptual modality to access energetic perceptions. That is why the memory fades. And why you need to record your dreams immediately.

Sometimes your spiritual self tries to counteract this fading effect by waking you at a moment in a dream that has a big emotional wallop. Or it gives you the same dream repeatedly. When this happens know that your spiritual self is trying very hard to draw your attention to an important issue.

This same intention applies when you have a dream that comes from a spiritual source outside you. An example is when someone from among your spiritual friends, your spiritual family, or your teachers or guides, communicates with you via a dream. One form that communication may take is when you dream of a person who is significant to you, such as a religious or authoritative figure. People report seeing Jesus, or Buddha, or Krishna, or a saint in a dream. They're not seeing that actual individual. What appears in such a dream is projected by a soul friend, guide or teacher, who use that authoritative figure to get the dreamer's attention.

Such communications are always to do with issues around life plans. Those in a non-embodied state usually step in to help and guide you when your spiritual self isn't getting the message through to your everyday self, or because before you incarnated those involved agreed that's what would happen at a particular stage in your life. The reason they do so is because they have a different energy to your spiritual self. That different energy, which is often stronger than what is available to your spiritual self, is brought in in an attempt to ensure the communication has a strong impact on your everyday self and that you therefore act on it. In these cases it is the power of the jolt rather than the subtlety of the communication that is the point. What those aiding you are trying to do is make you jump to it, and ensure you feel it is urgent that you jump immediately. As just noted, these types of communications usually occur at key times in your life, when a major turning point has been reached and when in order to fulfil a significant aspect of your life plan it is important that you undertake a specific course of action and not do something else.

These types of communications can also be directed to that portion of your spiritual self that is embedded in your human body. In another book in this series we answered a question on whether all of you is here. That chapter is relevant to what we are saying here. We observed then that only a portion of your full spiritual self is sent into the embodied state. The rest remains in a non-embodied state, watching and caring for its newest human identity. The portion of the spiritual self that is embodied is there to provide a dual awareness:

one level is the everyday mind centred in the brain and its cognitive system, the other level is centred in the awareness of the spiritual self. This means that your spiritual self is in you, right here and right now, perceiving and available to advise. But it can't always get through to you. In that case the non-embodied portion of your spiritual self steps in and offers guidance. If it fails, it then calls on others to help. That is the process we have just described.

When your spiritual self fails to get its messages across to you there are several reason this occurs. It may be that the spiritual self lacks experience. Human psychology is complex and it takes practice to negotiate its highways and byways. Or the embedded spiritual self may not be energetically strong enough to create an impact. Or the gloopy self may be dominating the individual's psychic make-up, crowding out the spiritual self's subtle signals. That is when energy is directed to the incarnated portion of the spiritual self, which then passes it on via a dream. The energy is experienced by the freshly woken person as a jolt, a jolt intended to get the individual to rise above its gloopy self and start doing the right thing by itself.

To speak of this process now in technical terms, these types of dream communications occur on several bandwidths simultaneously. The communication takes place within an electrospiritual bandwidth, because it involves one spiritual identity communicating to another. The individual's spiritual self then uses a dream to communicate to the individual's everyday awareness. It does so by using the electromagnetic bandwidth. Then, when the individual wakes remembering the dream, it is received by the individual's everyday mind which is operating within an electrophysical bandwidth. As can be seen, this is a multi-layered communication, requiring different parts of the individual's five-layered self to be plugged in. Those parts in turn utilise different modalities of perception and processing. You at the level of your everyday self will only be consciously aware of the dream jolt. What you remain unaware of is the extent to which parts of you are simultaneously using the electrophysical, electromagnetic and electrospiritual modalities. Yet without this multi-levelled passing on of energy you would not have a jolting dream to remember.

Now we arrive at what occurred during the dream described in the question. It has taken us some time to get here because we needed to lay down groundwork regarding not just the nature of dreams but how human perception works. This dream involves another perceptual mode again, different from any we have described so far.

We'll begin by discussing the quality of the dream. It was experienced as being much more real than is normal. The reason for this is because in dreams your awareness is usually passive. When you wake remembering a dream your awareness is detached. Usually, during your normal waking state, your awareness is wholly embedded in the electrophysical bandwidths of your self. In contrast, when you dream it is hovering in a psychic region that exists in the lower regions of the energetic self. There it can transfer easily back into the everyday electrophysical bandwidths, which it does when you wake. But it is simultaneously also open to electromagnetic inputs, which it receives via the energetic self. In this state your awareness hovers, open but passive. However, during the dream described in the question, the awareness was actively engaged. It looked around, thought about what was happening, and initiated an action. Dreams in which awareness is active have come to be called vivid dreams.

At this point we need to comment on the nature of awareness. Awareness isn't fixed. It is fluid. People train their awareness to be fixed, such as when they assert that the physical world is all that exists and nothing else. In this case they plug their awareness into physical reality. Nonetheless, they still dream, and their spiritual self still communicates with them, giving them nudges from time to time. And despite the fixed quality of their awareness, they often act on the nudges they receive. Of course, this is without being aware of, and certainly not acknowledging, the non-physical source of those nudges.

Others are more aware of the possibilities of their awareness. By undertaking exercises such as meditating, praying, repeating mantras or fasting, you can learn to consciously disengage your awareness from the electrophysical bandwidths and become open to other, non-physical perceptual modalities. Dreaming is one of these modalities. By consciously exploring dream states you can expand your perceptual possibilities.

As has been well documented by many writers, you can train yourself to wake up in the middle of a dream. What happens is that while you are asleep your awareness unplugs itself from your body's perceptual apparatus and plugs into your energetic self's perceptual apparatus. Its fluidity allows it to do this. Actually, your awareness is so fluid it can sustain physical, energetic and spiritual modalities of perception simultaneously. But that is another discussion.

To get back to what happens during vivid dreaming, your awareness wakes in the middle of a dream, becomes aware it is in a dream, and in that state it learns to function actively. That is, it can change the dream, skip back and forth along the dream's sequence, change the sequence, go somewhere else, or set a goal to achieve in the dream. Alternatively, as is reported in the question, the dreamer can throw a towel to shoo away a spirit. This is all possible when vivid dreaming.

Elsewhere we have discussed imaginal perceptions. These are subtle impressions you receive of non-physical modalities of perception. The impressions you receive while meditating, praying, doing yoga, listening to music, communing with nature and feeling a deeper pulse behind everything, each involve imaginal perceptions. *Imaginal* is not the same as *imagined*. Imaginal impressions are not the result of the imagination working overtime. Imaginal impressions are real. They are just real within non-physical modalities, which makes them subtle in comparison to the comparatively coarser impressions received via the body's senses.

People who have conditioned their minds to only accept sensory impressions as real struggle to comprehend that imaginal impressions are real too. This is why when people first become open to imaginal impressions they have difficulty deciding whether they are real. This is because imaginal impressions are so subtle compared to sense-based impressions, and because yearning for deeper communication can create projections that cloud the mind. It takes experience to learn to discern between imagined and imaginal impressions. Discernment comes as a result of becoming adroit in shifting perceptual modalities.

Ordinary dreaming and vivid dreaming are two modalities that exist within the total range of possible imaginal perceptions. Other imaginal modalities include encountering ghosts, having sexual relations with spirits (which is not as infrequent as you might think), and meeting all kinds of other spirits, some of whom might want to get to know you, most of which are indifferent to you, and a few of which are energetically so different from you that they give you a fright. This brings us to the topic of fears.

One issue that is not sufficiently discussed in metaphysical and meditation literature is that fear of the stranger is an ingrained human attitude. It is buried deep into the human portion of your awareness. So when you encounter something or someone with whom you are not familiar, and especially when their energetic signature differs significantly from yours, the response of human-based awarenesses is automatically one of fear.

Fear of the stranger became ingrained within the human psyche in the distant. Then people lived in small tribes. However, as populations grew, friction intensified, and a default attitude developed that those not from one's own tribe were potentially enemies. So when first meeting a stranger the response of suspicion became automatic. When suspicion expanded into a feeling of danger—and this was purely based on a feeling, not on whether danger was actually present or not—fear was triggered. Fear then kicked the adrenal system into action. As a result the individual either took up a fighting posture or ran away. This behaviour was so powerful because yoked what became an automatic socialised response of suspicion and fear to the automatic biological self-preserving behaviours of fight or flight. These have become deeply ingrained in the human psyche that all who choose to explore imaginal perceptions have to be aware of its presence and learn to overcome it. If you don't, if you let fear control your awareness, you won't get far in your explorations of imaginal perceptions.

These issues are relevant to the dream in question. To make the situation clear, the dream is one our scribe experienced. He experienced it because we put it there. To be even more specific, while he was sleeping we took his awareness into the electrospiritual bandwidth in which he could receive certain imaginal perceptions. We did this for two reasons. The first was for his benefit. The second was to add to the discussions in this book. In earlier chapters we introduced the idea that reality may be thought of as consisting of bandwidths. We also discussed non-embodied beings. Because we wish to extend our discussion of these two topics in relation to dreams, we decided to give our scribe a vivid experience that would lead to a stimulating question. This has happened, enabling us to respond to a depth we consider valuable.

To speak first on the benefit this dream has provided our scribe, we note that some time ago he learned first to wake up in his dreams, then to exercise volition while in the dream. He can change environments if he wishes, he can alter the sequence of what is happening, and he has learned how to withdraw from what he is perceiving if he becomes uncomfortable. He has not worked as intensely on his dreaming as those who develop expertise. Nonetheless, he has developed a preliminary level of skill. Without that we would not have been able to engage him in the type of vivid dream under discussion here.

In that dream there were actually only two active participants: our scribe and a non-embodied identity. In common parlance that individual is called a spirit. The term *spirit* is problematic in Western culture today. Either people believe there is no such thing, or else spirits are demonised, with people using the concept to scare themselves silly. Given this tainting of the word *spirit*, in the context of this discussion we won't use it any further and will instead adopt the term *non-embodied identity*.

So the only two beings in the dream were our scribe and a non-embodied identity. The rest of what our scribe saw was background scenery, sketched in to provide a setting. The friend our scribe recognised was not really there, but was represented in sufficient detail to be recognised. The gesture adopted by the non-embodied identity, of leaning over our scribe's friend, suggested some kind of vampirism was taking place. No such thing was occurring. The non-embodied identity was merely leaned over. But our scribe's own deep conditioning, which includes the fear of strangers we just described, led him to project his own fear onto the leaned-over gesture. That fear then spontaneously generated a vampiric image. As our scribe has experienced non-embodied identities attached to his energetic envelope, feeding off his energy, this was a plausible response. However, in this case, it was incorrect. In fact, we instructed the non-embodied identity to adopt this pose because we expected this would be our scribe's automatic response.

When the non-embodied identity sat back and smiled, it was really a smile of recognition. The identity was quite aware of our scribe's inward response. So the smile was half one of greeting to our scribe and half an acknowledgement that our expectation was correct.

Our scribe's perception that the non-embodied identity had a human body was another projection. This was a combination of our putting an energetic overlay around the identity that suggested a human body, and our scribe rounding out the suggestion. The fact the incident occurred in a house well known to him meant that he was primed to see the identity in human form. If, for example, the incident had taken place on another planet, in a setting that didn't resemble the human world, he would not so readily have interpreted our energetic overlay as human. He would instead likely have projected some other form on the identity, drawn from his memories of aliens in sci-fi stories.

It is necessary to appreciate the extent to which this kind of projection happens. There is an almost overwhelming urge for human-based awarenesses, when in non-everyday perceptual modalities, to interpret what they are perceiving into forms already known to them. This is what historical accounts of people seeing angels and elves involves. People see a non-embodied being, then, without consciously doing so, interpret what they see into human form. It is not that they are imagining the encounter. The encounter is real. They are just projecting a known form onto what is otherwise unknown. Because it is strange. And probably scary.

To give a balanced explanation of this process, non-embodied beings who regularly interact with human-based awarenesses sometimes adopt the forms of angels and elves to make those they are interacting with feel more comfortable. When fear enters the interaction communication usually ceases. Familiar forms like angels diminish the fear. But the human perceivers are not actually perceiving an angel. They are perceiving a projected overlay. This is another reason why you need to become aware of ingrained human fear, understand the extent to which that fear distorts your perceptions, and work on eradicating fearful responses from your psyche.

This, then, brings us to why this vivid dream was to our scribe's benefit. He now appreciates that his frightened response was wholly his own projection. There was no actual threat. Nothing untoward was occurring. If he had paused, quelled his fear, and smiled back at the non-embodied being, the interaction could have progressed into another modality. Instead, he chose to withdraw from the encounter by waking himself up.

The comment our scribe made about fright existing at the level of his energy self, and then transferring to his body, with the result that the hairs stood up on his skin, is wholly correct. For a vivid dream to occur, an individual's awareness needs to plug into its energetic self. That then provides what could be called an energetic body, which the dreamer uses to move, act and interact within the dream.

The bandwidths of vivid dreams vary. When dreamers fly over a familiar city or landscape they are using their energetic body to survey electromagnetic bandwidths of the physical world. In the case of our scribe's dream, he was engaged with another spiritual identity, so was using his energy body to interact on an electrospiritual bandwidth. Just as is the case with everyday interactions, interactions in vivid dreams involve plugging into different bandwidths and making use of different perceptual modalities.

How was this dream of benefit to our scribe? He now knows what goes on in such situations. Next time he will be aware of this and so will be able to work on reducing his automatic human fear response, the aim being to become more open to what is occurring.

We are not castigating him for this. Far from it. Learning involves repetition. When as a child you learned to walk, you stood, fell over, then tried again. This was repeated until you could remain on your feet. Similarly, when you learned to speak you tried repeating words you heard, didn't get them right, tried again. Eventually you became fluent. The same process applies to this type of exploration. Everyone gets better with practice. In the case of walking, it takes a few months to acquire sufficient skill. In the case of becoming adroit with using imaginal perceptions and interactions, it takes lifetimes.

To conclude, we wished to initiate a discussion of dreams because it was part of our plan that dreams be incorporated into this book. To repeat a point we made earlier, not everyone is able to use meditation to explore non-physical bandwidths of reality. Dreams are a viable alternative. This is because, as we also noted earlier, everyone dreams. We propose dreaming as a viable technology, alternative to meditation, for travelling into non-physical realms.

This discussion has had to be long because you, our reader, need a basic foundation for understanding what dreaming involves. We were able to spend considerable time in the last book discussing meditation, given meditation was that book's focus. We are conscious that this response is barely an introduction to dreaming. But we trust it at least establishes a coherent framework for discussing dreams. It is a topic we will certainly return in the near future.

Question 18

How much do we
create our own reality?

You say that as human beings we exist within a small number of all the bandwidths that constitute reality. We collectively perceive this physical world as real because we're all plugged into the same electrophysical bandwidths. Yet the situation isn't this straightforward, because our awareness is capable of shifting into non-physical perceptual modes, but not everyone does so. Consequently, we agree regarding the nature of physical reality, but we don't agree on what's happening beyond the physical. So the nature of what reality is for human beings ends up being questioned. Related to this, Seth, who was channelled by Jane Roberts, maintains that we create our own reality, collectively and individually. Could you clarify all this? And on the largest scale, how come humanity is plugged into this particular convergence of bandwidths, out of all those that exist?

THE GUIDES RESPOND:

This is another probing question, although it is couched in somewhat abstract terms. In answering it, we will focus on reality as human beings perceive it and construct it, because that is what the question is fundamentally asking: how is human reality constructed? However, before we answer we wish to dispel a false impression we may have given in our last response.

In answering the previous question we observed that fear of the stranger is a major reason people pull back from imaginal perceptions. Fear certainly causes this. However, fear is not the only reason. Another major factor is that exploring imaginal perceptions and their personal spiritual nature is not in everyone's life plan. Simply, many people have other things to do that are much more important to them this time round. For these individuals—and we are including the majority of humanity in this observation—it isn't fear but being busy with other things that stops them exploring the spiritual realm and imaginal perceptions. That in the process they ignore, limit, deny or ridicule spirituality and the imaginal mode is neither here nor there. When it is useful to them to do so they will address the spiritual aspects of reality that underpin their existence as human beings. Until then, their most urgent need is to deal with what they are faced with in their lives. And that is as it should be.

In practice, investigating your own spiritual nature is just one aspect of your development as a human being. Moreover, your development needs to be seen in a multi-life context. Just as you wouldn't expect an infant to run a cross-country race when it can't yet stand, so you don't expect people to delve into deep matters when they have their hands full dealing with the very real, compelling and important issues they face in their life. And, as we have observed elsewhere, even apparently loafing around, for an entire lifetime if need be, can be a very necessary time-out activity for individuals at a particular stage in their incarnational cycle.

Accordingly, we wish to make clear that not wishing to address spiritual matters is not always, and is even rarely, a matter of being too fearful to do so. Neither is being too occupied with other issues to focus on spiritual matters a signal of a limited or learner level of development. Even individuals who are reaching the end of their incarnational cycle may ignore spiritual matters for a lifetime or more. Because, as we just explained, they have other things to focus on.

With that clarified, we repeat that the comments on fear holding people back were solely intended to be understood in relation to exploring imaginal perceptions. Fear may lead you to misinterpret subtle impressions, conjure up non-existent threats, stop you in your tracks, or send you quivering back into your everyday awareness. In that context, fear certainly prevents people from exploring non-everyday perceptual modalities.

We hope that has dispelled a potential misinterpretation of our words. Elsewhere we have used the homily, different strokes for different folks. That applies here. Everyone has their own reasons for doing what they do, based on the life plan they organised before incarnation. There is no competition in this. There are no winners and losers. Everyone does what they have chosen, in the way they wish, at the speed that suits them.

Now we come to the question. To begin, we will note that the same comment we just made about fear and life plans also applies to people's differing notions of reality. In order to be committed to a life plan that involves high stake interactions and intense emotions, you need to be committed to physical reality. Given that, questions about whether a spiritual domain exists, and if so what perceptual modalities are required to access it, become irrelevant. You don't need to question the nature of reality. The very real life situations you are dealing with are what you need right now.

The point we are making is that a significant psychological factor is involved when you consider what reality does or does not involve. Focusing on the immediate physical and social aspects of human reality, when they are what you are enjoying, having problems with, or working your way through, are sufficient for your purpose, which is to learn and grow. You accept physical reality because it is providing what you need. For this reason people psychologically need not only to accept reality at face value, they need to lock onto the specific aspects of reality that enable them to explore what is important to them.

It may be said that people engage with reality on their own terms. They embrace what is important to them and block out what isn't. In this sense they are not so much creating their own reality as narrowing their perception of reality. This is a psychological necessity for two reasons. The first we have just described: it is because they have a life plan and need to focus on what is relevant to it. This means not engaging with, and often not even recognising, much that stands outside their life plan. The second reason we described in the previous response: the human cognitive apparatus can only handle a limited number of inputs simultaneously. As a consequence you ignore many of the sensory, emotional and intellectual inputs around you each moment because cognitively you can't handle them all. So when we say people engage with reality on their own terms, this is through a combination of personal choice, psychological make-up and the inherently limited human cognitive capacities present within you.

Could it be said that in focusing on what is important to you you create your own reality? Yes, certainly. But it needs to be understood that you create your own reality as much by blocking out impressions as you do by positively electing one thing over another. The very act of reaching out for one thing means you are ignoring everything else available to you.

Psychologically, each moment of each day you reach out towards certain objects, people, situations, possibilities and opportunities. They provide impressions. As you process these impressions you form a particular view of what is happening around you. This leads you to then reach out to the next thing, which provides you with fresh impressions. You then process these and use the extracted information to decide what to do next. In this way you are always rejecting certain possibilities while reaching towards those that attract you. As a result, you may turn a corner and something new suddenly becomes available to you. Or you may rechoose what you have previously experienced. Either way, you created that moment psychologically because your internal processing led you to reach out for it. So in that sense, yes, you are creating your own reality. But there's more to it.

The sciences have developed the concept of feedback loops. These form when output influences the next input. In the context of what we are discussing here, your output, in the form of the words you say, the emotions you share, the thoughts you act on, the choices you make, the activities you initiate or avoid making, constitute your output into the world immediately around you. That output puts you into certain situations in which others respond to you. When their input reflects your output, this is a feedback loop.

Of course, those others have their own feelings, thoughts and so on, that reflect their view of the moment you are sharing. So they may respond in ways that are outside your focus, providing new inputs that you hadn't previously considered, or that you don't want to consider—because people prefer not to shift outside their current focus. If this happens, and you reject new, alternative input, then you will remain inside your feedback loop, hearing, feeling, thinking and doing only what you are already hearing, feeling, thinking and doing.

Once people reach adulthood that is where many remain, looping through the same repeated inputs and outputs, over and over, without receiving anything substantially new. This is a crystallised psychological state, in which attitudes, feelings and notions about the world have hardened into a set perspective. Such a state keeps an individual fixed within a particular narrow notion of what reality consists of.

Individuals may become so protective of their narrow view of reality that they avoid any input that challenges it. By seeking only input that confirms their views they create what is known as an echo chamber. This is done out of fear, which is almost certainly buried deep inside them. However, the fear that is often apparent to others, who hear their defense for not accepting what doesn't fit their outlook, is usually secondary. The primary fear will be deeply buried. In this sense, seeking to sustain one's reality by living in an echo chamber is a psychological defence mechanism. We have discussed this process at some depth in the *Channelled Spirituality* books.

We repeat that yes, in the normal course of human interactions, everyone does create their own reality—or, more specifically, their own view of reality—through the feedback loops they sustain. From the perspective of development, the important issue then becomes that of stepping outside your feedback loops and opening yourself up to new input. Doing so enables you to create a new reality for yourself—or, at least, to create a perception of reality that is new for you. This is what spiritual development involves: breaking down all the crystallised behaviours, ossified attitudes, hardened assumptions, rigid outlooks, and psychological presets, in order to become open to new input of all kinds.

An unavoidable truth regarding this developmental process is that it can only occur step by step. Many people long for some kind of blinding revelation of Truth, involving some intoxicating enlightenment event, that will instantaneously and totally transform their view of reality. Unfortunately, this is not how development goes. You have likely seen sci-fi stories in which a person has vast amounts of data downloaded directly into her or his brain, then struggles to cope with it. The same applies in life. Picture having everything known about quantum physics downloaded into your mind. Quite apart from whether you could hold it all in without bursting, without preparatory training you wouldn't be able to make sense of the data. It would be gibberish to you. The same applies to spiritual input: you need to prepare for its arrival. And that is necessarily a step by step process.

Of course, this doesn't preclude ah-ha moments, when something clicks and you see an aspect of reality in a new light. These realisations certainly occur. When you work hard on an issue, attempting to understand what is going on, realisations will arrive. However, from our perspective ah-ha moments are incremental, even big ah-ha moments. When you receive them, process them, and absorb their lessons, they can change your orientation to the inner and outer worlds a little, or even a great deal. Near death experiences do this. So do insights obtained during meditation. Or when you are quietly communing with nature. Or when you suddenly see a person well known to you in a new light. These are all developmental steps, in which psychological feedback loops are transcended and you activate a new perceptual modality. This transformational process is what inner development aims to achieve. Accordingly, it is something you can engineer for yourself, through the active application of self-enquiry and related practices.

To conclude, from our perspective there is just one really significant point in all this: you can change your reality. By this we mean it isn't just that you can temporarily change perceptual modalities. What you can do is permanently change the way you relate to reality. What you perceive, how you process your perceptions, and how you relate to those you encounter—all this can be changed. You don't have to be locked into a psychological straightjacket. You don't have to live forever within the same feedback loops. You can change the way you function. And in the process you can make a new reality for yourself. As a by-product of your efforts, you can also change the way those close to you see you and, as a consequence, themselves.

The question states that everyone agrees they are living in the same physical reality. This is debatable. A dozen people could be standing together, sharing the same physical space, but one is enjoying the colours, another the smells, one is occupied with a phone call, and another is worried about someone not present and so hardly notices what is around them at all. So just occupying the same physical space doesn't guarantee that people are agreed regarding the reality they occupy. The idea of reality has a psychological dimension that makes physical reality different for everyone.

This also applies throughout the epochs of human history. Long ago people worshipped gods of place and offered sacrifices to nature gods in the hope of keeping storms and droughts at bay. Later the notion of the physical world being filled many gods was replaced by the notion of one God over all. But for some this God was loving, for others God was angry and punishing, and yet others felt God was ignoring them, and not in a way they felt was beneficial. So as people walked through marketplaces, or herded their goats towards feed, or sailed the seas in search of goods to trade, they shared physical reality with their companions, but all kinds of different notions were playing through their minds, leading each to interpret the same physical world quite differently.

In recent centuries the sciences have replaced religion for many, with the result that notions of material causes, chance and cosmic indifference play through their minds. Of course, while some assume the dogmas of science, others still believe in a loving or punishing God. Some may even believe in nature gods. And all these people could be sharing an airport waiting room, sharing the same physical reality but interpreting the world they share in very different ways.

To this extent we agree with the questioner. Human beings have always had contested notions of reality. Beyond basic motor-level agreement regarding the physical layout of a space, which prevents people from bumping into each other, there is little agreement regarding what reality is and where its limits lie.

Yet it is also true that people agree on the basic contours of physical reality. How is this? In part it is because physical features certainly exist. Streets, hills, the sky, beaches, the oceans, cities, deserts—they are there. A desert doesn't switch in and out of physical existence. A desert remains present even when—and we are nodding now to idealists— no one is looking at it.

On the other hand, everyone gets trained in how to perceive reality. Most people are born into a body with five functioning senses, which operate within certain bandwidths of electrophysical reality. These bandwidths delimit what you perceive. Yet everyone is trained how to use their senses from birth. Those born into hunter-gatherer cultures are taught to see, hear and smell things that urban dwellers do not. But urban dwellers can navigate malls and operate electronic devices with a facility traditional hunter-gatherers do not possess. So different kinds of expertise is developed in different cultural environments. Today, you have been trained from birth to function within the electrophysical bandwidths in certain ways and to utilise certain aspects of your capacities in specific ways. From infancy your attention has been directed towards some things and not towards others. In this way you entered an over-riding feedback loop that is constructed and sustained by the culture in which you live.

So how is it that humanity is plugged into this particular convergence of bandwidths, out of all those in existence? It is due to feedback loops. While there are slight cultural differences from one country to another, everyone is taught to utilise a certain number of bandwidths. Over time these have become standardised and accepted by human beings as constituting reality. But, as the questioner pointed out, this is merely an agreement that is taught to the young and then sustained through participation. Mutual affirmation generates feedback loops that keep everyone plugged into the same electrophysical bandwidths and perceptual modalities.

Is it possible for humanity as a species to change the electrophysical bandwidths it primarily uses during its physical existence? Of course. As we noted, individuals have long been doing so. All that is required is to disconnect awareness from feedback loops. Naturally, this is easier on an individual scale than on the broad population scale. But it will happen. We noted earlier that different species in the universe operate on different bandwidths to the human. Many species began with a limited sensory connection to reality, just like humanity, but genetically engineered their bodies, developed their cognitive capacities, extended their perceptual modalities, and now they freely function across a far wider number of bandwidths than was originally the case. Their everyday self has become vastly more complex, which allows them to utilise a much wider range of perceptual modalities than are currently available to human beings. It is possible that homo sapiens sapiens could one day become like them. Clearly, many changes need to be made before humanity could accomplish this, but it is a feasible goal.

In the meantime, and considering this is highly unlikely to occur within the incarnational cycle of anyone currently living in a human body on this planet, what we come back to is the notion that your reality, the reality you occupy not just physically and socially but psychologically, energetically and spiritually, is definitely something you can change, for yourself, and to your advantage. Treating reality as a developmental opportunity is certainly an approach to living that we recommend.

Question 19

Forget slow development, I want enlightenment now!

You say the point of being here is to use our life to develop, to change who we are step by step. That's easy to say but not so easy to do, because as I see it we're stuck with being who we are. Trying to gradually change ourselves just seems unrealistic. Pragmatically, how can we get out of who we are and develop into someone new? I would love to be transformed. But it seems to me that what we really need is a zap of enlightenment that will shock us into another mode of being. Forget slow development. What we all need is a bolt of enlightenment. Now!

THE GUIDES RESPOND:

Historically, enlightenment has been taught as what should be sought to gain spiritual insight. With this has gone the idea that those who become enlightened also become superior beings, worthy of being revered as great and wise. It appears that in emphasising slow development we are opposed to this viewpoint. We are. And yet we are not.

The main developmental arena in which enlightenment is taught today is Zen Buddhism. That spiritual tradition incorporates the experience of satori, awakening, as a a key part of its learning process. However, even among Zen Buddhist schools there is disagreement over whether satori occurs incrementally, over years, or in one huge moment. Either way, no one achieves a momentous satori by just turning up and sitting for an hour in a meditation hall. Years of practice is involved as students go through a series of breakthroughs as they follow the developmental pathway mapped out by Zen teachers. We could discuss all this in terms of feedback loops, suggesting the idea of satori is a construct that is sustained by all participants, teachers and students. This is not to say that satori doesn't happen, that it's an illusion. This is not what we are saying. Moments of enlightenment, which we earlier denoted ah-ha moments, do happen, and often. But no single great moment of enlightenment is going to transform you into a super-being like the Buddha. It's not how development takes place.

The idea that one magic moment is going to transform everything is deeply grained in the human psyche. A few years ago the idea was widespread that the planet would pass into a new transformational cycle in 2012. This was linked to the ancient Mayan calendar. In Indian mythology there is the concept of yugas, extremely long periods, which have different modalities, some better, some worse than what preceded. Because the Indian notion of time is cyclic they have the idea that the yugas will cycle and recycle forever.

In the West and Middle East time is seen as heading towards a transformational moment which is popularly known as the end time, when God will descend and transform the world. Because reward and punishment is embedded in so many religions, believers think they will be rewarded by sharing heaven on Earth with their God, while unbelievers will be sent to hell.

Even scientists, who do not believe in divine figures descending from the skies, have their own idea of a transformational ending, given many believe in the heat death of the universe. Where religious believe divine will powers everything, those scientists believe that thermodynamics, utilising energy, underpins everything. They believe that one day the energy will simply run out and, like a light switch being turned off, the universe will be snuffed out.

All these outlooks share the notion that there will be, in the future, one transformational moment in which everything existing will be suddenly transformed. What is the truth in such a notion? We would compare it to being a child at Christmas and feeling huge excitement, waiting for it to be time to open the presents under the Christmas tree, then being blissfully happy when the time finally arrives. This is the feeling that is embodied in the religious and spiritual traditions that teach that a single moment will transform human existence.

On the other hand, among those scientists who anticipate the heat death of the universe, the over-riding feeling is much more pessimistic. They are like the parents who organise Christmas for their children, who after the day is done sit back and say, "Thank God that's over." Those scientists' solace is that because they don't believe in the post-death continuity of consciousness, they won't be around when lack of energy causes the universe's lights to go out.

We are putting this somewhat humourously. However, as we see the situation, underlying all this talk of end times, yugas and heat death is considerable anxiety. The anxiety is that people aren't in charge of their lives, that there is a force external to humanity, whether that force be God or thermodynamics, that is ultimately in control. So all you can do is cross your fingers, wait for the grand moment, and hope you'll be on the right side of it. Even the spiritual notion of satori has this feeling of helplessness underlying it, that transformation requires something external arriving and transforming you. In Christianity the equivalent concept is of grace, in which God picks out someone and transforms their existence in a small or big way.

We don't wish to be perceived as being dismissive when we say this, but we suggest that such talk involves a childish level of understanding. Wanting a big moment of transformation is similar to being a child waiting for the presents to be opened on Christmas Day. It is a valid feeling. Who would not want children to have happy moments as they grow up? But as you get older your perspective changes—especially if you're the one who is organising the children's happy moments—and you come to appreciate how much hard work goes on behind the scenes to orchestrate the big event, none of which the children see. People have to be organised, money has to be earned to pay for the presents and the accompanying celebratory meal, the venue needs to be prepared before then tidied up after. The fact is that orchestrating happiness is hard work. Yet, and we are speaking now from the perspective of the adults who organise the day, watching the children's happiness makes it all worthwhile.

We suggest this is how you should view your own development. You are both the child and the parent. You are both the child who waits anxiously and excitedly for the day the presents will be opened, and you are the parent who actively and patiently organises the big day for the child. The big day for the child involves a big explosive moment of joy, while for the parent it involves a slow, incremental build-up. Both go hand-in-hand.

By asserting this we are agreeing that big moments occur in life. Birth, death, losing your virginity, being announced as a winner, being called into the boss's office to be fired, saying "I do", signing the divorce papers that announce "I don't"—these are all significant moments in people's lives that transform how they see themselves and how others see them. But behind every such moment there is a huge amount of organisation—biological, social, economic—that builds towards the big moment and makes it possible.

We add, there is also a great deal of anxiety around each of these big moments, with people wondering if they will fail to perform, fail to adequately support others, or fail to display the right stuff at the required moment. Yet the big moments come and go, and life carries on, taking you with it.

What about spirituality, then? Don't big moments have a significant role in spirituality? Certainly, they do. Everyone who works hard has memorable first experiences, when they were praying, meditating, or working on aspects of themselves, when things fell into place and their understanding jumped up a level. If people keep working hard significant firsts will keep occurring, and you will keep on having ah-ha moments. This is part of any skill building and developmental process. However, no one becomes a master builder or an Olympic athlete or a four star chef in a single moment. They work towards it. Similarly, no ah-ha moment will occur to you that is so huge it will immediately transform you into a superior spiritual person.

People like to repeat stories such as that the Buddha spent seven years sitting under a bodhi tree, and suddenly he had a satori in which all the scales fell from his inner sight and he became enlightened. There is a great deal of romanticism in repeating such stories. As the question makes clear, people often repeat them because they long for something similar to happen to them. What such longing ignores are the many prior lives during which the spiritual identity behind the Buddha—for the Buddha was a sub-identity of a far greater spiritual being—worked life after life developing different aspects of its awareness, honing skills, eliminating negative psychological traits and nurturing positive qualities, which collectively helped the development of its accumulated human identity into a mature individual who was loving and wise. To achieve that the spiritual identity engaged in hard work life after life.

Are you capable of achieving what the Buddha achieved? Actually, that is the wrong question. What should more properly be asked, and we are putting ourselves into the shoes of the questioner here, is: Are I capable of achieving everything that naturally accords with my inner nature? The answer to that question, of course, is yes. Why we say *accords with my inner nature* is that what the Buddha achieved was in accordance with his deep nature. What you have the potential to achieve is in accordance with your inner nature. Only the Buddha could be the Buddha, and only for that single life. Just as only you have the potential to become the future you. So if you use the Buddha as a model, it is not that you have to emulate what he did. What you are best to emulate is his application. He applied himself on a developmental trajectory, the ultimate purpose of which was to give full expression to his deep nature. You are advised to similarly apply yourself to developing what resonates most deeply with you. This naturally involves working to eliminate psychological traits that hold you back.

Do individuals get added help? Everyone gets help from those in their close spiritual circle. Sometimes help arrives from those who are further away, but if so this is part of their life plan. What people call moments of grace do not arrive arbitrarily, dispensed by some divine figure who decides, "Yes, I'll help this one but not that one." Rather, a moment of grace, to give help that name, is earned as a result of effort. To explain the process via a metaphor, earning a moment of grace may be likened to a fruit tree earning its fruit.

A fruit tree puts in hard work and as a result blossoms appear. By hard work we mean energy has to be drawn out of the local environment in the form of water and minerals, the energy is processed, then it is directed towards the tip of a twig, where in due course a bud appears and grows. So blossoms don't just arbitrarily appear at a certain time of the year; the tree works hard to produce them. Once the blossoms open up bees are attracted to them and the blossoms are pollinated. Pollination facilitates the final stage of fruit growing from the blossoms. Similarly, in the development of any skill, talent or insight, it is due to your effort that it blossoms and bears fruit. For that to occur you inevitably receive outside aid. The bee that arrives to pollinate the blossom could be seen as an moment of grace, a moment of satori, that arrives from outside to take the blossom to the next level. However, we suggest that what is involved is an entirely natural process.

Whenever an aspect of your life blossoms, as a result of you giving expression to a skill or deep trait, in effect you are opening up yourself up to new impressions, just as a blossom by the act of opening makes possible the arrival of bees. The bees carry pollen, and new impressions carry energy and information that provides you with further stimulus. Once the energy and information is processed, they contribute to you growing inner and outer fruit of various kinds. So it is not that you get singled out because you are special or chosen, just as the fruit tree is not singled out by the bee as special or chosen. The bee does what the bee does, which is to check out blossoms. Similarly, subtle impressions are around you all the time. But it is only when you manifest a delicate blossom that you are able to receive them.

Our scribe is fond of a saying from the Christian Gospels: "To those who have shall be given, to those who have not the little they possess will be taken away." This occurs regularly in life. If, say, a child is talented in a sport, they are noticed and much time, energy and resources are made available to them to develop their talent. A child who is not good at sport will not receive that same support. Is this a case of one child being picked out and the other rejected? Certainly. But the child is picked out on the basis of the work it has done. Remember that even if a child is naturally skilled in a sport by virtue of having an appropriate genetic make-up, they have chosen to be born into that body possessing those genes. And they chose the genes in order to extend the skills they developed in previous lives. So it is not that they arbitrarily possess the useful genes. And neither have they been picked out arbitrarily. It is all a natural blossoming of previous effort. Just as the bee arrives because the blossom exists, so opportunity arrives because they put themselves into the situation to have that opportunity and to take advantage of it.

What we wish to emphasise here is the role of personal effort. The more effort you make, the more you put yourself into a situation where the assistance you need to go to the next level will become available. The opposite can also occur. If you put yourself down, if you think you can't do something, then it is unlikely success will result. To return to the Gospel quotation, will "the little you possess be taken away"? No. That is exaggeration. What you have, you have. What you are, you are. What your accumulated human identity contains, it contains. No one can take that from you. However, you can take away your own future opportunities, in the sense that you reduce them for yourself.

People talk much about belief, and the need to have faith in what they believe. In general, we are not advocates for either beliefs or faith. Having blind faith, especially in beliefs others invented long ago, is not useful. However, believing in yourself, and having faith in your own capabilities, is certainly useful. Whatever you attempt to do, there will be periods when you don't seem to be getting anywhere and your goals are as far away as ever. During these periods it is beneficial to adopt an attitude of faith, believing in yourself and having faith in your own abilities, that you can get to where you desire to be.

People become discouraged for many reasons. You can blame others for not supporting you or even for holding you back. But it is your life. It is up to you to make the effort to achieve your goals. That requires you to keep making an effort even when your life looks bleak.

When your developmental goals are distant, it is easy to get depressed, or cynical, or pretend indifference, or engage in any of the many psychological strategies people adopt to justify why they haven't achieved to the level reached by others around them. To which we respond with just one word: application. You need application. Without application nothing can be achieved.

A principle that may usefully be extracted from the Gospel saying can be explained via the concept of feedback loops. When you are in a negative inner state, in which everything appears hopeless and futile, you ignore the positive impressions around you. Instead, you open yourself up to impressions that reinforce your hopeless outlook. Your negativity then forms an inhibiting feedback loop. Being in a funk, you shrug off anything positive others offer you and only recognise and accept negative inputs. It is in this sense that it could be said that "the little you possess", that being the possibilities existing around you, "will be taken away", i.e. through your attitude of rejecting positive impressions you are taking them away from yourself. Conversely, "to those who have shall be given" in the sense that if you have a positive attitude towards yourself you enter an amplifying feedback loop. Then you put yourself into positions in which opportunities blossom, and you receive impressions and energy that nurture what you are developing.

The questioner desires enlightenment in order to jump out of a self-limiting feedback loop. This is understandable. But it is not how development works. Each person has to start by making a decision to act, then consistently apply themselves. Whether acting involves reading certain books to expand their outlook, going to a course to learn a new skill, seeking advice on how to change their state of mind—whatever it may be—transformation begins with a decision followed by sustained action.

Make the effort, apply yourself, and you will certainly transform yourself. Have faith in your own potential. Apply yourself. Then blossoms will open within you and bees will arrive carrying ah-ha moments of insight and inspiration.

Can't we just do
what feels right?

I'm laughing to myself, because I have these little motivational cards on my window sill and one says, "Don't follow where the path may lead, go instead where there is no path and leave a trail!" Isn't life really just about listening to our intuition, and if it feels right going with it? What's wrong with that?

THE GUIDES RESPOND:

We have no intention of making you feel, our reader, after reading these pages, that you are not up to the task of self-development. We rather re-emphasise what we have already stated: you are best doing what you can, within the bounds of your life situation, at an intensity that feels comfortable. It is for this reason that we have been descriptive rather than proscriptive. That is, we have described in broad terms what self-development involves, but we have not stated categorically that you should or need to do this or that. You are the one who is living your life, and you are best to live it as you see fit.

However—you didn't think there would not be a *however*, did you?—if you have reached this final chapter we can assume that you have some interest in the task of bettering yourself, in whichever ways you consider betterment applies to you. This is why we have pointed out a few directions in which you who seek self-betterment may journey, but we have left it open for you to choose which particular direction and how far you wish to travel.

Nonetheless, we do urge you to choose at least one direction and commit to travelling at least a little way. Why? Because you have to face up to your limitations many times during the course of your incarnational cycle. This means that what you tidy up now you won't need address another time. Similarly, the skills you work on now, no matter how apparently minor, will function as building blocks, laying the foundations for greater achievements in years to come—years in this life, and in the many yet to be lived.

This multi-life approach to understanding why you are where you are is crucial. That is what we have been striving to impress on you, our reader. For you are not just you. You are not a one-off. You are many. You are part of a continuity of multiple identities that will keep experiencing, learning and evolving. If we were asked what is the one point we wish to make here, then this is it. You are on your way to something far more expansive than you currently know yourself to be. *That* is a concept worth committing to.

As regards following your intuition in all this, in broad terms we agree. However, we have some caveats. This is because intuition is a vague term which means different things in different contexts.

For example, intuition is often equated with a gut feeling. As inner perceptions go, a gut feeling is crude. People have a gut feeling when they dislike a person, or they feel he or she isn't to be trusted. Or after something doesn't turn out well, they claim, "I had a gut feeling that would happen." These types of feelings need to be interrogated. Often they are the result of prejudices, which in turn is the product of social conditioning that is racist, sexist or judgemental in some way. Political outlooks grounded in negative, discriminatory feelings, run on gut feelings. Clearly, we are not in favour of these.

As a side note, we observe that conscience is often aligned with gut feelings. People's moral attitudes are commonly shaped psychologically during childhood then subsequently applied to all situations, irrespective of the nuances involved. Life is full of nuance. There are many reasons why others do what they do. When people respond rigidly, without investigating what is involved, it is a good guide that what they are calling their conscience is no more than a collection of unconsidered gut feelings. Intuition can also be used to justify personal agendas. You may have a strong desire to do something, but another person gets in your way. So in your eyes they become a bad person and you tell everyone all about it. This is bias, not intuition.

On these grounds, we suggest that whenever you use what you consider to be your intuition, you interrogate what lies behind it, examine the circumstances in which you are applying it, and be very careful what you are using it to achieve.

This equally applies to situations in which you are deciding what to do next in a life situation. If your intuition pushes you in one direction over another, it is best to stop, take a deep breath, and re-examine what you are considering doing. In this case the best advice we can offer is to disconnect your awareness from your socialised self. Your socialised self is the part of you that is most shaped by your upbringing, so it is where most of your pre-sets, judgements and denigrating attitudes sit. These do also exist in your essence self, but to a lesser extent. Accordingly, we suggest a two stage process.

When evaluating an intuition, first disengage from what is happening around you. Engender a quiet inner state, then recheck what you are feeling. Is your intuition coming from deep down? Or is it more an instantaneous gut reaction? If you know it isn't a gut reaction, but you can't decide otherwise, that's a good thing. It leads to stage two.

Stage two involves seeking verification. This can be achieved in a variety of ways. One is to ask others what they think. Another is to meditate silently, then ask your deep self what it thinks. Another is, before sleeping, to ask your deep self for a confirmatory dream. Each of these could be repeated until you are satisfied that your intuition is correct. The important thing here is that you take a little time to let the intuition settle inside you and find out where it is from.

This might all seem quite contrary to what intuition involves, given it is, by definition, considered to be an immediate response that occurs without conscious processing. Nonetheless, if you are using your intuition to make an important life decision, then it is worth taking your time and ensuring you make the best decision you can.

For less significant decisions, trying to integrate your intuitive capabilities into your everyday life is a very worthwhile exercise. This is because it will enhance your sensitivity. To explain what we mean we will describe how we see intuition.

Intuition occurs primarily on two levels. The first level is within your essence self. This level incorporates your higher human moving, emotional and intellectual functions. This is where you experience in depth, process impressions, and learn. So if you make a snap intuitive assessment of a situation, and in doing so your awareness is centred in your essence self, then your snap assessment is drawing on your previous experience. An intuitive call made from this part of you may sometimes be wrong, but because it is grounded in experience it will often be accurate. It certainly won't be a crude prejudicial gut feeling. Accordingly, we would term this kind of intuition *an assessment based on experience*. It does have limitations, however. For example, a doctor may draw on prior experience to make an intuitive assessment regarding what ails a patient. But while the symptoms may echo previous cases, the causes may differ. Only testing will reveal this, and even then perhaps not if other specialists are not familiar with the alternative cause either. Accordingly, we suggest that intuitive assessments made at the level of the essence self still need to be verified.

Intuition in its purest sense is guidance that comes from your spiritual self. Such guidance is quiet, so quiet that it can take several years of practice to get sufficiently familiar with its flavour for you to recognise it when it arrives in your awareness. So even in this case we suggest you recheck deep within regarding an intuition, if only to ensure that you are interpreting it correctly.

We conclude this response with an affirmation. Yes, do what feels right. It isn't necessary to have a rational justification for why you want to do what feels right. Actually, few people use a rational process for making key decisions in their lives. Often an opportunity comes up and you just feel this is the one to go for. In that situation it is enough to pause inside for a moment and examine your feeling. If it feels positive and non-judgemental, then follow it. Sometimes such feelings also defy practicality. Again, if the feeling seems pure to you, it is most likely worth following.

We say "most likely" because everyone's situation is different. Writing here, not knowing our readers personally, and necessarily limited to making general statements, we can't offer definitive advice. Except this: Be kind you yourself and others. But do not indulge yourself in all things. Learn to be tough on yourself, but tough in a positive way, tough in the sense of challenging yourself to achieve greater things than you have, and so advance to greater heights.

Question 21

Having lifted the veil
a little, what's next?

Okay. Here I am, living my life and trying to figure out how to make the most of where I am and what I'm doing. You've offered a lot of insights into that. The first question in this book was: What is my purpose? What should I be doing? Let's go back there. Having had the veil lifted a little, and found out a little of what is going on, what should I do now? What's next?

THE GUIDES RESPOND:

The central purpose of enquiring into metaphysical issues, of seeking to learn about what is happening in your life beyond the purely physical, is not just so you can say, "Gosh, that's interesting." The real point is that you obtain a different view of your life and appreciate that they may be a direction for you to go that you didn't even know was there.

The human situation can be likened to existing in a valley. You have daily routes in which you, say, go to work, drop off kids at school, go shopping, go out for entertainment. On special occasions, such as visiting family or going on holiday, you might leave the valley and travel elsewhere. Travel is usually along established routes through the valleys. On special occasions you may even travel to a very distant valley. But this one valley is where you live most of your life.

A significant feature of valley life is that mountain peaks tower over everyone. Usually these peaks are swathed in clouds, so those in the valleys don't see them. But everyone is so busy with their lives that they don't look up much anyway. Besides, the peaks have no impact on anyone's life because everything people need is around them in the valley, so they can happily live without taking the peaks into account.

There's another significant feature in the valley. Under the valley floor are massive caves. These aren't a threat, no cracks or fissures are going to crack open, swallow houses, and disrupt life. Everyone is perfectly safe. Nonetheless, the caves are there beneath the feet of the valley dwellers as they go about their lives. So these are the three basic levels of life: the valley, towering mountain peaks, and subterranean caves.

Human beings have a great deal of curiosity. A handful among them are always exploring their environment and trying to figure out the what, how and why of their existence. Accordingly, people have discovered the caves and explored them. Now a handful of explorers run workshops about the caves, describing them in their many details. But some explorers have more experience of the caves than others, depending on whether they have travelled into them a short or a long way anf how frequently they have done so. In addition, some among those running workshops haven't actually been into the caves themselves. They repeat other people's stories about the caves, or just make up stories of their own. Some explorers run workshops in which participants get to descend into the caves. There are many entrances into the cave network, and quite a range of experiences are possible due to the huge variety of what exists down there. There are small ledges to balance on, narrow passages to squeeze through, huge caverns to walk around, glow worm grottos that create wondrous spectacles, streams and rivers to float down, pools to dive into that provide access otherwise hidden caves, and so on.

The people running workshops on the caves offer different types of experiences. Some just lecture on the features of caves. Some organise brief excursions into caves right near the surface, so the light of the overhead sun is never lost. Others take people into the darkness, where illumination is needed to explore. And some organise groups of explorers who travel a great distance through the cave network, even coming out somewhere different to where they went in.

Because there are so many features within the caves, all these diverse experiences are possible. And many more experiences wait, given only a small portion of the total network of subterranean caves has ever been explored.

All this means that those running workshops about the caves have very different levels of experience and knowledge. The same variety exists among the valley dwellers regarding the caves. Some valley dwellers deride those who are interested in the caves, maintaining there are no caves, it's all just imagined jiggery-pokery. Others are happy to hear about the caves, wonder at the stories told by those who have entered them, but they don't want to explore the caves themselves. Others definitely want to experience the caves, but to varying degrees of engagement. Some are content to enter just a short way, without leaving the sunlight. Others aren't satisfied with that and want to journey deeper. Some of those want a boisterous experience, like white-water rafting in the blackness. Others prefer the glow worm grottos, where they can have a quiet, wonder-filled aesthetic experience. Others want to investigate sounds they hear, wanting to see the creatures that make them deep in the caves. Yet others are so adventurous they set off in ones or twos and are only seen again years later, or not at all. These represent the varieties of attitudes towards the caves and the levels of personal engagement with the caves.

The same range applies to the mountains. Many people believe super-beings live on the peaks and worship them with lesser or greater intensity. It is notable that these worshippers don't go up the mountain slopes to worship the super-beings, preferring to build churches in the valley and worship down there. Others don't believe in super-beings, considering them figments of the worshippers' imaginations, projections their desires map onto the world above them. Yet others say they've never seen the peaks, so don't accept the peaks exist, let alone super-beings who supposedly live on the peaks. Then there are those who not only believe the peaks exist, they gather equipment for climbing and go exploring. As in the caves, some climb a little way while others ascend a great distance. Some climbers claim they have seen super-beings, others never see anything. Some return frightened, discovering they don't have a head for heights. Others return buzzing with excitement and want to go up again as soon as they can. Yet others encounter storms or avalanches and come back injured, or even die high on the slopes, never being seen again.

Of course, this is a metaphor for your situation as a human being. Your feet are planted on the valley floor, which represents this physically and socially constructed world. As for the caves and mountain peaks, they exist within you and around you.

The caves represent your deep self. There are portions of the cave very close to the surface. This is your biological self, which includes all your bodily and immediate cognitive functions. A little deeper is your socialised self, consisting of those parts of your psyche shaped by external events. Deeper again are the higher human functions of your essence self, made up of the practical, emotional and intellectual modalities of your being. Shifting among these are two aspects of personality, false personality and true personality, that we haven't discussed here but are explored in *Psychological Spirituality*. Deeper again are the energetic self and the spiritual self. All these parts speak inside you, variously shouting or whispering. Most people are more comfortable with the shouting, because they've spent their lives listening to those voices and have become used to them. The deeper selves speak very quietly and are often drowned out. Sometimes people hear sounds that are so foreign they think they are being made by something scary, a marauding creature, even a monster. Of course, they're not. What they're hearing are aspects of their selves, but ingrained fear of the stranger causes them to project their anxieties onto the sounds. The only stranger present is a deeper aspect of their own self that is unknown to them at the level of their valley-dwelling self.

The mountains and their peaks represent non-physical bandwidths of reality. Ascending into them isn't for everyone. Many prefer to keep their feet firmly on the valley floor. In order to justify their preference, numerous people deny that non-physical bandwidths exist. Others worship them without entering them. Yet a significant number of valley-dwellers do put on their hiking boots and explore the slopes. As with the caves, some ascend further and some are content walking on the lower slopes.

At this point our cave-valley-mountain metaphor breaks down. This is because in order to explore non-physical bandwidths of reality you need to shift into non-physical modalities of perception. And to do that you need to enter into yourself, tap into capabilities beyond the purely physically focused, and draw on the perceptual modalities available to your energetic and spiritual selves. In other words, you need to descend into the cave in order to ascend into the mountains. The further into the cave of your self you enter, the greater access you'll have to the mountain bandwidths.

Where does this fit with what you should do next? Our reply is, do what attracts and that you feel comfortable with. There is no stigma regarding how far you do or do not explore. It is up to you. However, we offer a few observations.

First, everyone can challenge themselves to go further. If you can go one step, you can go two. If you can go two steps, you can go three. But there is no rush about this. Go at your own speed. Just don't say to yourself, "This is far enough, no more." There is always further to travel. There is always more to perceive.

Nonetheless, we add to this that sometimes you need to pause and digest what you have experienced. Sometimes you need to take a breather and think about the new information you have acquired and integrate it into your view of reality. Processing may require you to read pertinent books, attend relevant workshops, consult illuminating experts. Get other people's views on what you have experienced. Understanding is often best achieved communally, by sharing experiences and observations. That way you will come to see a particular experience from a variety of perspectives. The resulting understanding will generally be more balanced and nuanced than if you take your own experiences as definitive. Consulting and comparing will help ensure misperceptions and exaggerations don't skew your understanding.

Second, start with the humdrum stuff of your daily life. In order to go deeper within, your awareness first needs to descend past the socialised self, then beyond the essence self. Both have limiting traits in them. These need to be addressed because otherwise they will impact negatively on your deeper perceptions. So anything psychologically that bugs you, that you notice turning up in your life repeatedly, direct your attention towards it first. Identify it, understand it, and work to diminish then eliminate it. We outlined the process for doing so earlier in our discussion of self-enquiry. It starts with keeping a journal, then makes use of an analytical framework for understanding what traits are impacting on your life and how deeper they are buried within. Further details on addressing negative and self-limiting traits are provided in the *Channelled Spirituality Series*.

Third, learn to trust your deep self. Adopt a regular practice, whether that involves meditation, internal silent prayer, dreaming, yoga, silent communing with nature—whatever practice works for you—and use it to make contact with your spiritual self. The aim is to hear its very quiet voice. Then develop a rapport with that voice, becoming so familiar with it that you can pick out its gentle whispering among all the other internal voices that capture your attention during daily life. Once you have learned to hear it and trust it then you can say you have established a relationship with your inner guide.

All this occurs within the context of your life plan. So, fourth, delve into the circumstances of your life, as well as into the nature of your identity. Doing so will take the sting out the tough aspects of your life, and will also enable you to become more satisfied with what you achieve. No matter how large or small the tasks are that you have set yourself, it is satisfying realising that you are ticking them off.

All this involves coming to appreciate more deeply who you are, why you are here in the circumstances that constitute your life, what your goals are, and who these other people are who are helping you achieve them. We repeat, digging down into this level of understanding will make you feel much more satisfied with your life, and so much less frustrated, than you most likely currently do.

Naturally, all this is occurring as part of a series of lives. You have your hits and misses, wins and losses. This is a natural part of learning. But as we said, if you fail at something, put it down to experience, pick yourself up, and take the next step. That is what you are here to do. This is what being human is all about.

With that we bring this book to an end. Until next time, we bid you farewell.